Social A

Overcome social anxiety & shyness forever!

Jennifer Alison

Copyright © Jennifer Alison Publishing

All rights reserved.
No part of this publication may be reproduced, distributed, or transmitted in any form or by any means, including photocopying, recording, or other electronic or mechanical methods, without the prior written permission of the publisher, except in the case of brief quotations embodied in critical reviews and certain other non-commercial uses permitted by copyright law.

About The Author

Jennifer Alison received her doctoral degree from Illinois School of Professional Psychology in Chicago and her Masters degree in Applied Psychology from the University of Baltimore.

Jennifer Alison specializes in the treatment of anxiety disorders and related physiological issues and has published several papers and books on this subject as well as speaking at conferences around the world.

Jennifer Alison divides her time between New York and London with her husband Stephen.

Table of Contents

It's Time To Overcome Social Anxiety

In today's world, around 40 million Americans are affected by anxiety disorders, a large portion of whom struggle with social anxiety. The amount of pressure that many of us are under at work and at home seems to be constantly increasing. We are expected to put in more hours and more effort all the time. Society is competitive these days, ruthless at times, and life can be extremely stressful. The truth is, most of us will battle some form or anxiety at some point in our lives. It's not something that's reserved for people with poor mental health. Anxiety is a natural process that usually occurs before, during and/or after stressful events or major life changes. But nowadays, social anxiety is on the rise, and it's not just affecting people who are going through something devastating or catastrophic. In fact, many people develop social anxiety out of nowhere and their experiences range from feeling slightly awkward in social situations to being riddled with panic attacks, social dread, and depression. Many of us prefer communicating to others via text or email rather than enduring face-to-face conversations. We might simply prefer to stay in rather than going out for an evening. We might cling to our personal comfort zones for dear life. But unfortunately, the more we avoid social interactions, the harder they become.

Whether you have a fully debilitating case of social anxiety disorder or you just feel a little uncomfortable in social situations, this book is for you. Social anxiety is something that anyone can overcome, no matter who you are or how badly you suffer from it. Permanent change is possible. Anxiety itself is not always a bad thing. It functions as your body's natural response to environments or situations that are dangerous or threatening. In this way, anxiety can be quite helpful. If you're being physically threatened, anxiety will cause your body to produce adrenaline and trigger your fight or flight response. This gives you the extra strength and heightened awareness you need to fight off danger or run away, even if you have been injured. But unfortunately, when we experience anxiety, our bodies may produce adrenaline when we don't actually need it, and this can be problematic.

For instance if you're riding the bus and you feel crowded or you run into an acquaintance on the street and they insist on engaging you in a *"stop and chat"*, your brain might overreact to the perceived threat and tell your body to start getting ready for a fight when there is really nothing to fear. You might end up feeling nauseous or lightheaded. You may tremble or feel like your heart is going to leap out of your chest. You may experience a full-blown panic attack. And what's worse, most people who experience episodes like this could find social situations increasingly difficult as time goes on. In order to free ourselves from social anxiety, we have to learn how to turn off the fear and stop our bodies from producing that extra adrenalin, or else we risk becoming more and more fearful of social encounters. This can of course, mean that our quality of life will suffer.

Social anxiety doesn't just affect people at large social gatherings. It can cause crippling bouts of nervousness, apprehension, and panic in the face of simple everyday activities as well. This means that even things like shopping, going to work, visiting relatives, talking on the phone, and virtually any other activity that involves other people can be agonizing. It can put unnecessary strain on friendships, intimate relationships, and relationships with work colleagues. It can take the enjoyment out of your life, replacing it with panic, grief, and feelings of low self worth. Living in fear can cause stress, depression, missed opportunities, physical ailments, and general malaise. But it's important to know that you do have a choice in the matter. If you want to beat social anxiety, you can. If you want to free yourself from panic attacks, you can. If you want to be able to go out on dates or simply have a face-to-face conversation with someone without sweating or thinking you might throw up, you can!

One of the best things about human beings is our ability to grow and change throughout our lives. We all have the potential to be happier and healthier regardless of who we are or where we come from.

When dealing with social anxiety, it's important to think about the times we live in. These days, as a result of the rise in social media usage and the amount of communication we engage in via text and email, we are working towards a completely dehumanized society.

The more we communicate with people behind the safety of our computer screens, the less able we become to comfortably experience real life interactions. Therefore, as social media culture rapidly becomes "the norm", it is no great wonder that so many of us find socializing in "real life" as anxiety provoking as we do. Online, we have the opportunity to present ourselves exactly the way we want to and this often means that our true selves remain hidden.

We present a version of ourselves that we want other people to see. We take time to make sure our responses to emails and texts make us look smart, funny, and light hearted. We edit ourselves again and again so that we don't offend people or say something we might later regret. But if we spend this much time perfecting our online socializing, it's only natural that we'll feel uncomfortable when we're forced to think and speak on the spot. Plus, if you never get the opportunity to be your true self and to be comfortable with that version of you, is it any wonder that so many of us experience impending feelings of doom, self loathing, fear of failure, and low self-esteem?

Human beings *need* to socialize. We have a fundamental need to be part of groups. We need to feel valued and approved of. We need opportunities for love and affection, camaraderie and support, togetherness and care. Living in isolation doesn't just make you feel lonely. It can affect your mental health, your self-beliefs, your physical health, and even your life span. It can add negativity and pressure to your relationships. It can lead to unfulfilled potential and unrealized dreams. Living life on your own can make you question your true purpose and cause you to feel hopeless.

The amount of people suffering with social anxiety is growing constantly and I intend to explore and challenge the reasons behind this change throughout this book. However, it is my personal belief that the dominating force of social anxiety in today's world means that we need to make a conscious and persistent decision to change the way we socialize. Replacing human contact with technology can be of great benefit in some avenues in life. It can make business transactions faster and smoother, and we can all get more done in a day by sending a few texts rather than having to meet everyone face to face. However, if we replace *all* of our social interactions with screen-based communication, we will only grow more socially awkward as time goes by. If we don't challenge ourselves to connect with people in the real world, we will likely experience even more nervousness and self doubt as a result.

How many times have you wanted to go to an event but ended up staying in because you felt uncomfortable or nervous? When you do that, do you wake up the next morning feeling good about staying in or are you disappointed that you missed something you might've enjoyed? Do you feel embarrassed or angry with yourself when you choose not to show up to a social event? How are your relationships with friends and family members being affected by your anxiety? Are there people in your life who are altering their behavior to make things easier on you?

For instance, does your partner agree to stay in with you when they really want you to go out with them? Have people stopped inviting you out because they know you won't come? How is your social anxiety contributing to your feelings of self worth? How is it affecting your enjoyment of life? Are you able to date and/or make new friends? Are you able to maintain healthy relationships?

Do you feel like your life revolves around panic attacks or anxiety about upcoming social events? Is your anxiety causing difficulty at work? Do you have difficulty planning outings or vacations? Do you experience difficulty with every day activities like shopping, attending appointments, and running into people you know on the street?

Most importantly, *are you happy or is it time for a change?*

No matter who you are and to what degree your social anxiety is affecting you, there is hope. By seeking to understand your anxiety and challenging yourself to break free of it, you can completely and permanently overcome it. Social anxiety does not have to define you. It doesn't have to maintain its hold on you, nor must it continue to shape your life. Our time on this earth is limited enough. We all deserve to enjoy our lives. It's never too late for us to learn new things, take on new challenges, and improve our quality of life. Say no to social anxiety and start reclaiming your life now. You deserve it.

Social Anxiety and The Solution

Like many fears and phobias, social anxiety varies considerably from person to person. But no matter how anxiety features in your life, this book will cover everything you need to know to kick it to the curb. Social anxiety can affect anyone at any age. It can be anything from mildly annoying to completely debilitating. It can cause you to feel awkward or petrified. It might lead to total avoidance of social situations. If it is allowed to get the better or you, social anxiety can cause depression and even agoraphobia. It can be hugely disruptive to your life. If you've bought this book, you probably already know what social anxiety feels like for you and how it affects your life. For this reason, and in the interest of focusing on the solution rather than glorifying the problem, I will keep this section brief and to the point.

It is important for you to understand that all types of anxiety are rooted in fear. And when it comes to fear, anxiety does not discriminate. So whether your fear is rational or irrational, whether it's rooted in fact or fiction, as long as it's allowed join the party, you can bet anxiety will be there with bells on. Being able to identify what you're afraid of is an important step toward obliterating your anxiety and throughout this book, you will be encouraged to do just that. But for now, take a moment to read over these three lists about what social anxiety looks like and how it could be affecting your life. Make a note of any signs and symptoms that you experience or identify with.

Physical Effects
Sweating
Dry mouth / Excessive thirst
Upset stomach
Increased heart rate
Clamminess
Feeling too hot or too cold
Restlessness
Feeling an urge to use the toilet
Headaches and/or jaw pain

If you suffer from panic attacks, you may also experience the following
Hyperventilation
Dizziness
Shortness of breath
Muscle twitching
Feeling as though you are having a heart attack, stroke, or seizure
Feeling as though you are losing control or making a scene
Trembling
Tingling in your hands, feet, or face

Behavioral Effects
Babbling or talking too fast
Freezing up or not talking enough
Scratching, fidgeting, hair twisting or other compulsive grooming
Difficulty making eye contact
Discomfort eating in public
Constantly checking the time
Indulging in "safety behaviors" such as insisting on sitting near an exit, always having water with you, or never going anywhere alone
Using your mobile phone as a crutch i.e. looking at your phone so as to appear more relaxed or busy when you're feeling uncomfortable in a social setting
Missing out on events you would usually enjoy
Missing out on meeting new people and/or dating
Avoiding social situations completely
Disengaging from the social events while you're there or purposefully not joining in
Regularly changing or canceling plans
Relying on social media, texting, and/or emailing for the majority of your communication with others
Self sabotage i.e. not showing up for job interviews or important meetings, ending intimate relationships prematurely, or missing events that are important to your friends and family such as weddings, birthday celebrations, and funerals

Mental And Emotional Effects
Dread or worry about upcoming events

An inability to slow down your racing thoughts
Difficulty concentrating or following conversations
Focusing too much on your fears or your physical symptoms
Experiencing paranoia i.e. believing other people don't like you or as if they are talking about you
Catastrophic thinking and focusing on worst case scenarios
Fear of sitting in enclosed spaces, such as a window seat on a bus or the middle of a row in a movie theater
Fear of running into someone you don't want to see
Feeling like you're in the spotlight
Fear of being criticized
Stress about meeting new people
Stress about being in the company of authoritative figures
Feeling awkward, uncomfortable, or as if you don't belong
Becoming easily embarrassed or ashamed
Internalizing negative feelings and dwelling on them
Feelings of low self worth or poor self-confidence as a result of a recent change such as gaining weight, going through a break up, or losing your job

As I said just moments ago, anxiety is rooted in fear, as are many other difficult emotions. But how exactly do you develop social anxiety? Learning to identify your fears in order to understand what you are feeling and why, could be one of the most valuable lessons you will ever learn. Many of our more challenging emotions are a mask for something else. For instance, when we feel angry, there are almost always layers of other, more difficult emotions hiding beneath it; such as rejection, fear, nervousness, inadequacy, insecurity, confusion, grief or sadness. Anxiety is similar to anger in that, very often, it is covering up a deeper feeling. Anxiety has a way of taking center stage while our other thoughts and feelings get pushed to the back row.

When you are able to identify and explore your hidden emotions, coping with them, *and* the anxiety they cause, will become much easier. In order to this, you must get into the habit of actively asking yourself questions about your feelings and behavior. You must reflect on how your feelings and behavior contribute to your social anxiety both during and after social events. This way, you will be able to identify why you experience the degree of social anxiety that you do; and from there, you will able to start fighting it. Most of us aren't used to this type of thinking so it will take time and plenty of practice before it becomes second nature. However, once you're in the habit of regularly reflecting like this, you will naturally become less anxiety ridden. Your dread and apprehension will recede. I will refer to this way of thinking a lot throughout this book, and I encourage you to think of it as *being curious*.

When we think about ourselves and the people around us with a *curious* mind, we are opening ourselves up to a deeper level of knowledge; we are seeking to understand our feelings and behavior so that we can guide our thoughts into safer, healthier territory. So too, when we are curious about other people's feelings and behavior, we are less likely to succumb to catastrophic thinking about what they think of us. We are less likely to be consumed by paranoia and self-doubt. Thinking like this has the power to build healthier, longer lasting relationships. It can make your communication with other people more balanced, productive, and enjoyable. Most importantly, it can help you develop a healthy sense of self, a higher degree of self-confidence, and less anxiety across the board. This is a large part of what we are aiming to achieve with this book and it's possible for anyone.

Case Study: Rebecca

When I first started talking to Rebecca, she was riddled with social anxiety and had recently started experiencing agoraphobia. Her self-esteem was low and she had reached a stage in life where she was completely alienated from her friends and family. She was lonely and felt trapped in a miserable life.

Rebecca wasn't always like this. She was once a very sociable woman with a large group of friends and a tight knit family. But everything changed when she lost her job. Having never been fired before this, Rebecca hit an all time low. She had loved her job; it was a source of great pride in her life. She'd enjoyed what she was doing with her life, and her self-esteem was heavily dependent on it.

So when it ended, it felt like her world had come crashing down. She went through a long bout of depression. She was mortified and ashamed, and that led her to push her friends and family away. She just couldn't face them. She didn't want their advice or their sympathy. She chose instead, to wallow alone. Time passed and, having done all they could to support her, eventually people stopped getting in touch altogether. Even though she knew that she had been making things harder on herself by pushing people away, she still felt scorned and rejected when they were gone.

I was surprised when Rebecca set her first goal because it seemed so simple. All she wanted was to be able to walk to the grocery store without being petrified of running into someone she knew. The more I talked to her about this, the more I realized just how much she struggled with this particular fear. She didn't want to have to engage in a spontaneous conversation with someone on the street. What if they didn't know she'd been fired and they asked her how things were at work? She didn't want to have to admit that she'd lost her dream job. But there was also a deeper fear beyond that. Her self-esteem was in a fragile state and she was terrified of being "blanked" on the street.

We have all been in this situation. You're walking down the street and you see someone you know walking towards you. You get butterflies in your stomach because you're caught off guard and you haven't prepared for the conversation. But then the person keeps their head down and walks straight past you. You're left wondering, did that person blank you because they don't like you? Did you say something to offend them at some point without realizing? What did you do to cause this?

This line of thinking can be really dangerous. It's one sided and entirely self-focused. This is where "being curious" comes in. Rather than wondering what we did to cause this, we need to be able to think about what the other person may have been thinking and feeling in that moment. Maybe they were having a bad day. Maybe they were sick or sad. Maybe they were feeling nervous about engaging in conversation too or perhaps they were just running late.

Maybe they were wrapped up in their own thoughts and they didn't even see you!

For Rebecca, learning to be curious about other people's thoughts and feelings was a huge break through. Since she had been consumed by anxiety for so long, she was basically trapped in a bubble of her own experience. She was tortured with paranoia about what other people thought of her. She felt like a failure and she was afraid of being judged. But after learning to be open to other people's thoughts and feelings, rather than thinking their actions were directly related to her, Rebecca was able to free herself from a large part of her anxiety.

She had to accept that even though she had taken a big hit to her self-esteem, that didn't necessarily change the way other people had felt about her. In fact, once she got the chance to rebuild her relationships with friends and family members, she found out that the opposite was true. The people she'd pushed away were still there for her. They were there to support and comfort her. They wanted to help her get back on her feet. All she had to do was value herself and her life enough to let them.

Human beings are immensely complex. Everything about us is unique. All of our thoughts, actions, and self-beliefs are a direct result of our individual experiences and our genetic make up. For this reason, each of us will have our own causes and triggers lying beneath our anxiety. Have a look at the next two lists and once again, make a note of any causes or triggers that you think might be responsible for your social anxiety. Are any of these things contributing to your avoidance of social situations?

Dealing With The Causes

Poor social skills or difficulty sensing other people's tone or intentions
Difficulty conversing due to limited practice
Fear of embarrassment

Fear of catastrophe or always focusing on what could potentially go wrong

Fear of being judged or rejected

Fear of being misunderstood or disapproved of

A difficult relationship history including those with friends, family members, and intimate partners

A difficult or abusive childhood

Low self esteem or lack of self-confidence

Feelings of low self worth or insecurity

Negative self-beliefs

A personal or family history of mental illness

A personal history with specific phobias or compulsions

Being judged by unreasonably high standards including those which are self inflicted as well as those placed upon you by a partner, family member, or employer

Being introverted or shy

Obsessive or catastrophic thinking including excessive worry

Difficulties being assertive

Problems with addiction

A need for control

Fear of the unknown or the unpredictable

Dealing With The Triggers

A dislike of your appearance especially after a recent change such as gaining weight or being ill

A tendency to focus on your imperfections

Unexpected changes in life such as having a new child, going through a break up, the death of a loved one, or financial struggles

Feelings of inadequacy particularly after experiencing a loss such as losing a job or partner

Being bullied by co-workers, friends, or family members

Feeling left out or as though you exist on the "outside" of social groups

A genuine dislike of social situations

Failure and the potential for failure

Feeling unimportant, under valued, under qualified, less educated, or of a different social standing than your peers

Feelings of defeat following a rejection or failure
Fear of attention
Being near someone who intimidates you
Having to attend social occasions alone
Being in places which you connect to bad memories

Take some time now to look back over your lists. Give yourself 15 to 30 minutes to reflect on the causes and effects of your anxiety. Remember that the lists I've provided here are only a guide. Feel free to think further into your own personal experiences and write down anything else that comes to mind. Start to identify any reasoning behind your anxiety and allow yourself to reflect on any recent or past experiences that may have informed the way you feel about social situations.

Was there someone in your life who made you feel inadequate? Is there someone in your life now who is antagonistic or insensitive towards you? Did something happen that you found hard to bounce back from such as the loss of a job or the ending of a relationship?

Have you always had trouble socializing or is this a new thing? Is your social anxiety getting worse as time goes on? Do you hate having too much attention placed on you? If so, why? Does your anxiety have too much power over you?

What are you *really* scared of?

Asking yourself questions like this can be emotionally activating so please make sure to take things slowly and to treat yourself well during this process. If at any point you feel as though you are becoming upset, set this task to the side and come back to it when you're feeling stronger. In general, try to get used to thinking more deeply about your anxiety when you're in good form rather than trying to make sense of it when you're in the heat of the moment and your mind is racing. Remember that anxiety is personal, so the more you understand about *your* anxiety, the better equipped you will be to overcome it.

The Nature Of The Beast

Learning to think critically about your anxiety and being curious about it can feel pretty intense at the start. You might feel like you're forcing yourself to face things that you don't like about yourself or your life. You might feel like you're reopening old wounds at times, and if that is the case, it's important to be kind to yourself and not to push yourself too hard. Self-progression is a journey, not something that happens overnight. Anyone who claims to have a "quick fix" for anxiety is ignoring the investment and dedication it takes to make a lasting change.

Remember that it's important to take good care of yourself during any period of self-exploration. Make time to actively do things that are solely for the purpose of self-care. Take relaxing baths, go on long walks, read a good book, whatever it takes to make you feel happy, respected, and loved. Learning how to properly care for yourself and realistically assess your value in the world is a vital component of a healthy mind. By being kind to yourself, you are actively changing the way you think and feel; you are learning how to be productive rather than self-destructive. It's easy for us to beat ourselves up, but developing healthy habits can be a little more challenging. And when it comes to anxiety, knowing how to praise yourself can mean the difference between having your self esteem soar and having it bottom out. Before going any further I must stress, if you struggle with extreme bouts of depression or you are thinking about harming yourself in any way, please seek professional help immediately.

There is a terrible phrase that people use regarding a number of physical, emotional, and mental concerns. They say, *it's only in your head.* We've all heard it at one time or another and I cannot help but challenge this reductive condescension. Not only do human beings possess a deep and proven mind-body connection, but our "heads" are also the center of our very being. Our brains control everything we do! They control our breathing, our movement, our pain response, and our perception of the world around us. If you've ever attended a social outing with someone who is particularly outgoing, they may have told you that you're being paranoid or that you just need to lighten up and have some fun. *It's all in your head!* Unfortunately, even when your friends and family mean well, phrases like this can make you feel even worse about yourself and make you dread social situations even more. The idea that things that are "only in your head" can just magically disappear is about as reasonable as putting a Band-Aid on a severed leg and thinking you'll be able to get up and walk again. The things that are in your head are there for a reason - whether they are justifiable or not - and they are not always easy to shake off.

Think about *placebo effect* for a moment. This phenomenon is so *real*, that when testing out the effectiveness of new drugs, doctors must give a certain percentage of patients a placebo so that they can measure the true effect of the drug versus the effect the human mind can have on the illness. I personally think of placebo effect as the ultimate mind over matter experience. The idea that our minds are so powerful that they can actually cause physical change is truly incredible. There are people in the world who have overcome illnesses and/or eradicated the symptoms of illnesses by simply *believing* they could. If what goes on in our minds is so strong that we can actually overcome physical illness by tapping into it, surely what happens *in our heads* is pretty powerful stuff. And if this is the case, one can only deduce that your anxiety, paranoia, and dread of social situations is very real indeed.

When I talk about the nature of the beast, I really do mean to liken anxiety to a monster. It can grow and change as much as you can. It can feed on every negative experience you have and every moment of self-doubt. It thrives on weakness. When you are low, your anxiety is high. Whether you are crippled with nerves or you simply feel a little out of practice in the social sphere, anxiety is there waiting to pounce. But you may have noticed that when you are high, your anxiety is more likely to be low. When you are strong, anxiety is weak. And the more you understand anxiety, the more it recedes.

It's important to be able to recognize if and when your social anxiety is flaring up because you're in a period of low mood, rather than falling into patterns of believing that something is *wrong* with you.

Living with social anxiety can skew your judgment. It can mess with your perceptions. You might think that you're weird or crazy because everyone else seems to be having fun while you're hiding in the bathroom splashing water on your face. Everyone else seems to find it so much easier than you, so much more enjoyable. But if you're in a period of low mood or you've had a particularly rough night out, you're more likely to go home and dwell on your shortcomings. You'll be unkind to yourself and think about how you stood out for all the wrong reasons. If that is the case, is it any wonder your confidence might suffer as a result? Is it any wonder your anxiety might be even worse the next time you tempt it?

When you learn to view yourself through more realistic eyes, when you learn to lift yourself up rather than putting yourself down, *then* things will really start to change. I will visit this topic again later but try to keep this it in mind as you progress. Try to notice any times when you're being unkind to yourself or being unreasonably hard on yourself, and try to turn your thinking around.

I often liken the monster of anxiety to addiction. This might seem like a radical idea at first but if you, or someone you're close to, has struggled with addiction, you might be able to see some similarities. Both addiction and anxiety lessen your potential. They can both ruin and run your life. They can cause similar downfalls and pose similar challenges. Both inevitably make your life harder. But anxiety itself, is also addictive by nature. It's something we get used to, something that becomes part of our routine, something that's hard to imagine living without. For instance, imagine you - like many others - get anxious on public transportation, but you have to take the bus to work everyday.

In the morning you wake up, shower, get dressed, have breakfast, grab your anxiety and head to bus stop. It's part of your *routine*. While you're on the bus, you might develop a habit of counting down the bus stops or distracting yourself with a book or a game, but all the while your anxiety is there with you. What would it be like to leave your anxiety at home? It might feel as strange and unusual as going to work without getting dressed. How do we break the *habit* of anxiety; the *addiction* we have to it? What would our minds focus on if not on our nervousness?

Despite the fact that anxiety is by all accounts, a negative experience, becoming addicted to it is as possible as becoming addicted to any other form of self-harm, and that includes alcohol and substance abuse. Where an alcoholic might reach for a drink, anxiety can very quickly become your "go to" fix for any new or difficult social setting. What would your life look like without anxiety? Can you picture it? Can you imagine being free of it? Wouldn't it be wonderful if your "go to" emotion was excitement or joy? Wouldn't it be great to be able to walk into the world with openness rather than feeling constricted and closed off?

For some of you, thinking of anxiety as an addiction might seem a bit farfetched, but for others, this could be a light bulb moment. If you have many different types of anxiety or you feel like you're nervous most of the time, you might be addicted to your anxiety. The idea of being powerful enough to let go of it might seem implausible. You may have tried every tip and trick available on the internet and read every book on the subject and still feel like anxiety has a hold on you. Even if you want rid of it, it can be easier to hold onto anxiety than it is to let it go of it. This is what you are battling. Yes, it may be "in your head", but anxiety is real and it is powerful.

Shyness

Before moving on to the next section, I'd like to encourage you to think for a moment about shyness. Not all people with social anxiety are shy, and not all people who are shy will have social anxiety. It's important to be able to recognize the difference between the two. If one of these things plagues you, you are not destined to end up with the other. However, some people do get hit with the double whammy and end up being both shy and uncomfortable in social settings. This can be a pretty major obstacle to overcome.

Shyness can affect people for a variety of reasons. Past experiences such as embarrassing moments, strained relationships with friends and family, or growing up in the shadow of a sibling can contribute to shyness; however, it's important to accept that many people are simply born to be more introverted than others. Shyness can be a real pain to contend. There may be people who will use your introverted nature as a way of putting you down. They might consider your ideas less important or less valid than their own. You might have to fight to be heard when surrounded with people who are more outgoing than you. Most importantly, being shy isn't going to be of great assistance when it comes to getting over your social anxiety. But, being shy is not a flaw. It is not something you should be embarrassed or ashamed of, and it's not something you have to change.

Try to think of shyness as something you can work with, not something you have to fight against. You never have to try to be something you're not and you don't need to become an extrovert just because you'd like to socialize more comfortably. Being shy can be quite an endearing quality, especially when you're surrounded by friends and loved ones. Plus if you've been shy your whole life, people that know you well enough might be able to help you through some of your more daunting social experiences.

There will always be people in our lives who are less than understanding about our individual hurdles. There will always be people who will insist that you just have to "get over it", but comments like these should be taken with a pinch of salt. It can be hard for people who aren't shy to understand your struggle. Just be careful that you never use your shyness as a stick to beat yourself up with. It is not the cause of your social anxiety nor is it your fault.

Dealing With The World Today

In the introduction to this book, I mentioned briefly how certain societal changes have rewritten the ways in which we communicate with one another. In this section I will expand on that idea and encourage you to think more deeply about how these changes influence you and/or affect your anxiety. Nowadays, most of us use text, email, and social networking sites for the majority of our social interactions. And although there are a number of undeniable benefits of using this style of communication, it doesn't come without its problems. Generally speaking, the amount of practice we get to actually talk to people face to face is declining rapidly. We rarely take the time to even speak to one another on the phone anymore. Furthermore, the older we get, the less likely we are to try new things and make new friends. But without practice, our social skills can get a bit rusty. The more you avoid something, the harder it gets to do it. So it's natural, to some extent, that social anxiety is on the rise.

When we communicate behind a screen, we have ample opportunity to edit ourselves. We can show all of our best attributes and keep our flaws and weaknesses close to our chests. But the more we hide who we really are, and the less opportunity we have to be our true selves, the more likely we are to experience low self esteem and self doubt. Take a minute to think about your friends on social media. Are there some people who are particularly vibrant online? Do they seem like their lives are almost perfect? If so, how do their posts make you feel? Is it accurate to say that many of us will feel intimidated, agitated, or slightly under confident when we're constantly exposed to a relentless feed of other people's near perfect lives? Might these thoughts and feelings be even further magnified if we happen to be in a period of low mood at the time?

When you are faced with these acutely edited, glossy versions of other people's lives, it's hard not to feel like their joy is a reflection on your discontentment. When reading other people's tales of triumph, it's hard not to be reminded of your own shortcomings. Moments like this have power to ramp up your social anxiety, *and* make you feel bad about it.

Furthermore, if there are people on your social media feeds who seem to dwell on the more negative parts of life, their moods can be contagious. Being exposed to sadness, tragedy, outrage, and harrowing news reports on a daily - or even hourly - basis, is bound to have an effect on how you feel. It's only natural to assume that if you are surrounded by anger and sadness all the time, you too, will begin to feel angry and sad. Being able to recognize when this is happening is extremely important when it comes to protecting your own emotional wellbeing. So, the next time you're scrolling through your feed and you start to feel like your mood is turning sour, it might be wise to take a break and shake it off before commencing with your day.

One interesting and oddly comforting thing about the world today is that, when it comes to social anxiety, you are certainly not alone. When you are out at a social gathering, you can take solace in the fact that the vast majority of people in the room are going to be focused on their *own* experience and their *own* fear. Very rarely will they be thinking about you. So in a way, even if you do something embarrassing or you say something less than smart, statistics show that most people won't even remember your faux pas by the end of the night.

Think about the word "awkward" for a moment. How often have you heard this word in recent years? The Awkward Movement has basically been a worldwide celebration of the collective experience of social anxiety. Memes were created to make light of social awkwardness, TV shows were aired. It was almost in fashion to be awkward for a while! This in itself is undeniable proof that the majority of people today know what it feels like to live with social anxiety. They know what it feels like to be overrun with nerves, to have panic attacks, and to want nothing more than to stay at home with a bowl of popcorn and do their "socializing" online. Sometimes just having that thought in your mind is enough to make you feel more comfortable in social situations. There is safety in numbers.

One thing worth keeping in mind is that we are the first generation that has had to navigate the art of socializing in the wake of the

Internet. These changes in society have been rapid and relentless. Dating has changed. The definition of the word "friends" has changed. Because of the nature of online communication, we have become impatient when it comes to conversation. When we send an email or a text, we want a response immediately. The anxiety we feel when that ominous dot, dot, dot flashes before our eyes, informing us that a response is being drafted, is proof that we need instant gratification to maintain our self worth. When someone takes a long time to get back to us, or they don't reply at all, our self-esteem will drop and our self-doubt will soar.

We become instantly worried and our mood can plummet in mere seconds.

What are they typing and why is it taking so long? Wait! Why did the dot, dot, dot just disappear?! Are they angry? Did I upset them? Are they rejecting me? Text me back so I can feel validated and be free of this worry!

It's like walking on a social tightrope. Suddenly other people (and their phones) have so much more power over how we feel about ourselves. And this all just because of *how* we talk to each other, let alone what we're actually saying!

Texting is complicated and it can be stress inducing. While some of your friends will reply immediately, others may sit on a text for a few days or even weeks before drafting a reply. The whole thing gives us way too much opportunity to overthink everything we send and receive. When you're speaking to someone in person, you'll never be able to remember the whole conversation word for word and there's something quite positive about that. Reading and re-reading texts over and over again, and dissecting them in search of any potential subtleties, can be torturous! Yet so many of us do it; especially when we are involved in a conflict.

These are times when we are already in a heightened state of emotion, yet we insist on torturing ourselves further with this useless behavior! And the worst part is that in texts, we can't accurately judge a person's reaction or tone. Without being able to see their face and hear the inflections in their voice, it's often impossible to know exactly what someone meant in a text.

The interesting thing is that the way we perceive texts is more likely to be affected by how *we're* feeling as opposed to how the other person is feeling. If you're in a period of low mood or you're having a bad day, you might read every text you receive as condescending, rude, or accusatory. By contrast, if you're feeling like you're on top of the world, the same texts could be read as funny, supportive, and kind. The fact that this type of communication keeps us on such emotionally flimsy ground, makes it a minefield for our self-esteem.

Furthermore, if you are the type of person that's great online - funny, smart, whimsical - what does it feel like when you're out in the real world and you can't edit yourself? Suffice to say, relying too much on screen based communication can add a ton of pressure to real life interactions.

In addition, life online has made us a lot more critical of ourselves and others. Everything we do - as long as we post it online - is available to be critiqued by every person we've ever met (and some people we've never met!). We are in constant competition with each other. We make fun of people for what they post online. We envy people. Like that person who is so vibrant online; and then there's the one with the perfect home; and that family that's always on vacation; and the happy couple with the straight A kids… It's a rat race of personal contentment. And of course all of this impedes on our own self-beliefs. All of it adds fuel to our anxiety's fire.

So what can we do about this? We can't exactly ignore these technological advances - our lives depend on them nowadays - but we do have to protect ourselves somehow. I personally believe that it is unnatural and unhealthy for people to be able to "see" you and/or contact you at all times. We shouldn't have to live under a microscope. We all need privacy and quiet time. We need to be able to value ourselves and our needs; to take care of ourselves and judge our feelings and actions realistically. If you know that social networking and/or texting is causing you added stress and increased social anxiety, take a break from it.

Stepping away from social networking is a good exercise for everyone to do periodically. It can help stop the constant chatter in your mind and help you to feel more grounded in yourself. You don't have to delete all of your accounts if you don't want to and you don't need to make a big announcement about it. You can always go back online when you're feeling recharged. But being able to recognize when you need a break is paramount to keeping social anxiety at bay. If it's texts that are bothering you, put your phone away for a few hours or even a few days.

This can be a very helpful practice if you're going through a conflict or a break-up; especially if you're prone to dwelling on the negative or thinking obsessively. It's too easy to scroll back over hurtful texts or stalk an ex online. If you do have a tendency to torture yourself in this way, ask a friend or family member to hide your phone for the day and tell them not to give it back to you until a designated time. Allow yourself to be alone with your thoughts. Do something you enjoy. Bake a cake, take the dog for a walk, play board games with your kids. Let your mind relax and breathe while you get some perspective.

It's no great secret that our children and teenagers need support and guidance when it comes to Internet bullying and coping with the pressures of social media. However, we adults could also use some guidance at times. Most of us grew up believing that when we reached adulthood, all the social pressures of high school and the agony of drama fueled relationships would be a thing of the past. Unfortunately, that is not always the case. Some people we meet throughout our lives are competitive by nature; others are inherently cruel or hurtful. Personal conflicts are never easy and they happen to us all. Furthermore, some of us have a tendency to put ourselves down because we are led to believe that other people's lives are all sunshine and lollipops. When people online seem to be walking on air, we can struggle to see the good in our own lives.

Believe it or not, without putting up some boundaries to protect ourselves emotionally, socializing online can cause depression, self doubt, cynicism, anger and frustration, low self-esteem and a variety of other undesirable emotions. And to top it off, any one of these emotions can cause social anxiety. The thing is, the Internet isn't going anywhere anytime soon, so if life online is affecting you negatively, it might be wise to build up some defense. For your reference, I have listed here a brief run through of things to keep in mind when it comes to staying safe online.

Staying Emotionally Safe Online

1 - Recognize when your thoughts and behaviors are harmful.

If you often feel drained, angry, or upset after spending time on social media, something probably isn't right. There are a plethora of reasons we might experience negative emotions about the things we see online. If you have low self-esteem for example, seeing people who appear to "have it all" may be making you feel worse about yourself. If you've recently gone through a break up or you just lost your job, going online to stalk your ex or your old colleagues is hardly going to make you feel any better. If you find yourself dwelling on other people's posts, comparing yourself to others, or thinking mean or nasty thoughts about yourself or other people, it might be wise to take a break from the internet for a little while.

When it comes to social anxiety, bad habits online will certainly not make things any better. Going online to see your ex with their new partner will not make you feel good about yourself, nor will it make you want to go out and be social. Continuing to return to social media when you know it's going to upset you is emotional self-harm. And if you want to get over your social anxiety, getting to grips with these compulsions is imperative.

Start by recognizing if social media is causing added stress or anxiety to your life.

Do you experience negative feelings during or after you've been online? Do you often return to someone's page repeatedly even though you know it's upsetting you or making you angry? Do you "stalk" anybody online? Do you think social media is causing you to have low self-confidence, low mood, or increased social anxiety?

Once you've taken some time to think about these questions, set some rules and boundaries for yourself. Start by disallowing yourself to visit anyone's page that you know will upset you. If possible, block or unfriend them to get rid of the temptation. Then set a certain amount of time that you that you think you should spend on social media each day and don't go over it. As a guideline, try to keep your online time under one hour per day if at all possible, with no more than two hours per day being the maximum.

If possible, take a break from social media entirely for a week or two, or give yourself a few full days where you don't go online at all. Next, make a decision about what you would like to use social media for and stick to it. If you'd like to have it so that you can be close to friends and family, use it that way. If you use it for news articles or interesting videos, try to limit your online experience to those things. Keep yourself safe by resisting posts or people that can hurt you. And anytime you start to feel agitated while online, switch it off.

2 - Practice realistic and positive thinking.

Don't believe everything you see online! It can be very easy to think that someone has a perfect life if all they do is boast about it online; *especially* if you're not feeling great about yourself at the time. Try not to think in grand sweeping statements like, "So-and-so has the perfect life", "So-and-so is always out at parties. They're always having fun. They're always happy", "So-and-so is always showing off and bragging about their kids", "I'll never have a life like that". This is a very black and white way of thinking and therefore, it's bound to be pretty unrealistic. No one is happy all the time. Everyone experiences hardships, difficulties, and triumphs. Life is full of ups and downs, no matter who we are.

Similarly, if you are prone to judging or mocking people online, knock it on the head. Spite is not a very gracious quality to possess, and it breeds negativity. When we think about other people with an "us versus them" state of mind, we're setting ourselves up for a fall and we're likely to become bitter and resentful. This way of thinking can also make you go into relationships and social events with a chip on your shoulder; thus adding another obstacle on the social spectrum that you will later have to overcome. Try to think about who other people are at their core so that you can better relate to them, rather than considering everyone an enemy. When you do find yourself thinking about other people in a negative light, remember to *be curious* about what they're thinking and experiencing. Maybe that person who's always out at parties has social anxiety too. Maybe they've worked really hard to get over it and they're celebrating. Or maybe they're depressed and can't bare being alone. Maybe that person who's always bragging about their kids had a bad childhood and is overcompensating for it. Maybe their relationship with their spouse is strained. Maybe they're just proud of their kids and it has nothing to do with you at all! Remember that people are complex.

Some people need an audience and that's why they spend so much time posting their lives on social media. This could be because they're under confident or it could be because they think they're awesome. At the end of the day, what happens online is not a comment on you or your life. Live and let live, and don't let it get under your skin.

3 - Keep it light.

As a general rule, try to keep your posts light and on the positive tip wherever possible. There are people who use social media as a negative sounding board and it's easy to understand why. It can be hard to express negative feelings to actual people in the light of day. Online, we have a chance to hide behind a screen and say all the nasty, rotten things we've been thinking but haven't been able to express. This can be an ugly cycle to stuck get in. Picking fights with people online isn't exactly likable behavior, and it rarely accomplishes anything other than attracting negative attention. Similarly, posting heavy or forceful political or religious beliefs can easily lead to scandal and conflict, not to mention upsetting people who happen to have opposing beliefs. So too, posting long and detailed accounts of your medical illnesses or personal dramas can be tacky and make people feel uncomfortable.

Of course there are times when things of a negative nature will be happening in your life and it's okay to reach out to your friends for guidance and support. But if your online profile is dominated by negativity, it could cause problems for you socially. If you know that you struggle with social anxiety, the last thing you want is for people to not want to be around you! So try to keep it light online and resist the temptation to get into heated arguments or fits of passion behind your screen. Leave your accusatory tone at the door.

Keep in mind that you might run into someone on the street who you've just had a conflict with online and you don't need to add any extra fuel to your stop and chat anxiety. In general, if you want to keep your reputation in the green, try not to say things online that you wouldn't say in person.

4 - Get clarity

We all know that if you're speaking to someone online or via text or email, tone and intention can get lost in translation. Body language, facial expressions, and voice intonation all play a massive role in effective communication. Without these crucial elements, conversation can get a bit sticky at times. We can get caught in traps of overthinking or dwelling on what someone *might've* meant by what they said. We can keep rereading the messages, show them to other people to get their take on the situation, and agonize about it, but none of these things are productive in any way. Patterns of overthinking can drive you out of your mind, and it's best to get out of them before things get out of hand.

So before you break up with your girlfriend or end things with your best friend because you feel offended by something they've texted, get some clarity on the subject. If you're unsure of someone's intentions towards you or you feel as though you may be misinterpreting something they've said, ask them what they mean! If things are still unclear after that, consider talking to them on the phone or ideally, meet up face to face. Resolving conflict is a lot easier when we can accurately judge the thoughts and feelings of each other. Goodness knows, we don't need extra obstacles when times are tough.

5 - Delete triggers.

This is one piece of advice that I can't stress enough. If there are people or messages that are upsetting you, draining your confidence, or causing you stress and frustration, get rid of them. If you have texts or emails that are hurting or haunting you, delete them. If there are people causing you stress or pain, delete their numbers and block them online. I realize how hard it can be to do this. If you have developed an attachment to someone, blocking them can feel harsh and very *final*. But if you continue to regularly visit their page or reread old texts and emails from them, you will never be able to move on with your life.

In my experience, deleting these triggers is the best way to move on and regain the ability to focus on yourself. Experiences from the past do shape who we are to some extent, but they do not have to define us. It is hard if you still love someone and they don't feel the same way - whether it's an ex-lover, an old friend, or a family member - but torturing yourself with memories isn't going to make getting over them any easier.

If you feel that you aren't ready to fully delete or block someone, take baby steps. Reduce your exposure to your triggers gradually if that's easier for you. Rather than blocking them, try unfollowing them instead. That way you'll still be "friends" online but their posts won't pop up in your feed all the time. Resist the urge to visit their page at all costs. That behavior will only hurt you in the end.

If it's texts or emails you're holding onto and rereading obsessively, it can be hard to face deleting them. It is natural for us to grow attached to these things, especially if they're evidence of a happier time. But if you want to be happy in the present, letting go of the past is a powerful way to help you get there. If you really think you can't handle deleting all of your old messages, think about filing them away somewhere where you won't be faced with them every day; and don't let yourself open that folder!

Keep in mind that these habits are not necessarily *bad*; they just aren't always helpful when it comes to moving on. Reducing your exposure to them will help you regain some personal stability. When it comes to getting over social anxiety, you might have to do a few things to boost your confidence. So if you have online triggers like these and they are causing an increase to your anxiety levels, you can't afford to hold onto them much longer.

6 - Maintain perspective.

As you know, life online can lead to obsessive thoughts and behaviors. We can dwell on so-and-so's updated relationship status, constant reminders of upcoming events, posts that we find particularly emotionally activating... The whole thing can be all consuming at times. But there comes a time when we've got to get some perspective. No matter what's happening online, real life continues to go on outside of our screens. Overthinking or dwelling on what's happening online can be really detrimental to your mood so it's important to keep your emotional feet on solid ground. If you're prone to dwelling or obsessing about things that are happening on social media, try not to let your mind run away with you and don't take yourself too seriously. Look in the mirror and tell yourself that you need to lighten up.

Most importantly, if you're involved in a conflict online, don't let it destroy your spirits. One great thing about life online is that it moves a lot more quickly than real life. When something happens online, it might engage people's attention for an hour, a day, two days at most, and then it's over. All will be forgotten and something else will take its place. It's a funny little perk of being part of an impatient generation. So whatever it is that's bothering you online, think of it like a storm: It'll blow over in no time.

Case Study: Nicole

When I first started talking to Nicole, she was going through a painful break up. Just a few months before she was due to get married, she discovered that her fiancé had been cheating on her. In the end, he'd left her for his mistress; a younger woman who possessed many qualities that Nicole had often wished she'd had. It was devastating. Her self-esteem was obliterated overnight. Everything she had planned for the future disappeared. She cried endlessly, desperately trying to figure out what she had done wrong.

But as if things weren't hard enough, Nicole focused on the other woman a lot. Online, she studied her face, her body, her past; always looking for reasons her ex had chosen to be with her. What did she have that Nicole didn't have? She obsessively checked both of their social media pages to see what the happy couple were up to. Here was a selfie of them on the beach... There was a post about their new apartment... Their new puppy... Their wild Saturday night. Nicole was becoming bitter and depressed. But she kept checking those websites, refreshing those feeds.

Her relationships with her friends became strained. Some of her friends were still friends with her ex and for some reason they insisted on telling Nicole how lovely this new girl was. Others just pitied her. There was no one she could talk to. People still invited her out but social anxiety had its claws in her. Life online had become so upsetting that the thought of rejoining the real world was terrifying. She couldn't possibly go out and risk seeing her ex with his new girl. Plus she was embarrassed. She'd had to cancel her wedding! She was a failure. She'd been blind. Facing the outside world became more and more frightening. She started having panic attacks at work. She struggled with the commute. Eventually she had to go on sick leave. But being at home alone all day and night meant having even more time to stalk her ex online.

Nicole's behavior wasn't making things any better, nor was she making things any easier on herself. She had become her own saboteur, and social media had become a tool for emotional self-harm. Yes, she had been hurt by her ex and it wasn't her fault. But when it came to coping with the break up, she was doing things all wrong. She was using life online as a way to stay rooted in her pain. Unknowingly, she was doing everything she could to prevent herself from moving on. She had to make some changes.

It took a lot of courage and a strong resolve but Nicole knew that if she was ever going to be able to get back into the world outside her apartment, she had start by getting away from the internet for a while. She started by blocking her ex's online profile and deleting all the texts and emails she'd been obsessively rereading. It wasn't easy, but once she took that first step, things slowly started to get better. She knew that she had to face the outside world again or she'd never get back to her old self.

Gradually, Nicole began seeing her friends again. It wasn't easy; her panic attacks made socializing difficult and this was hard considering she'd never struggled with anxiety in the past. So she took things slowly. In the beginning, she only met one friend at a time and always met them in quiet locations or at home. She resolved to take better care of herself physically and emotionally. And in the end, she got her life back. Things weren't exactly the same as they had been before the break up, but she got to a place where she was okay with the fact that she'd been vulnerable and she'd been hurt. She didn't beat herself up about it anymore. She knew it wasn't her fault. She accepted that she was just human, and she'd been emotionally knocked down. Hard times would come and go but in the meantime, she deserved to enjoy life.

Avoiding The Cancel Culture!

There is another facet of life in current times that I believe is increasing our overall social ineptness. I like to call it, *Cancel Culture*. In today's society, we have more opportunities to avoid social interactions than any generation before us. The sheer amount of plan canceling that happens nowadays is astounding. It's just become the done thing. We say to our friends, *"Let's get together and catch up soon!"*. We make plans via text to meet for lunch, and then the night before that lunch date, we send a text to cancel! And let's be honest, most of us do our canceling via text because it's a lot easier than calling our friends on the phone.

It is true to some degree to say that canceling has become socially acceptable these days but it does not come without consequence. If you're a chronic no-show, it's imperative that you take some time to think about why.

What is it that you're avoiding? If you're canceling doctor appointments, meetings with co-workers and classmates, or outings with friends, what is it that's driving this behavior? When someone shares an event with you online, how many times do you click the button saying that you'll be there? How many times do you actually show up? Why do you accept invitations when you know you're not likely to attend? Do you find it easier to cancel or simply not show up rather than saying no to an invitation in the first place? If so, why?

The thing about constant canceling is that it's a very easy habit to get into. When you send a text to your friend apologizing for missing their party, you don't have to see the disappointment on their face. You never really know what you missed by staying in for the night. Canceling is so common now that it's easy to get used to doing it. The problem is that the more you cancel, and the more you *avoid* social interactions, the worse your social anxiety will become. The day after you cancel, you might be left wishing that you'd had the courage to attend. You might end up beating yourself up for letting your social anxiety win again. You might start to feel alienated from your friends. You might feel like you're just "different" from other people and going out just isn't for you. If this sounds familiar, it's time to make a change.

Start by thinking about why you're canceling.

Are you canceling plans for genuine reasons? Are you feeling too nervous to attend or are you actually self-sabotaging by creating distance between you and your friends? Do you really want to go out but you just can't seem to get out the door? Are you so comfortable in your own company that you dread being around other people? Are you afraid of being judged? Under confident about the way you look? Are you nervous about discussing a recent change in your life such as an illness or a death in the family?

Take some time to think on these questions and try to be fair and honest with yourself. There will probably be more than one thing here that strikes a chord with you and there may be other factors in your life which I haven't listed here. Identifying the feelings beneath your canceling habit is a big step. It will help you to understand if, when, and why you are avoiding certain social encounters.

Reflect on these things a few times as you progress through this book. Try to identify any behavioral patterns or thought processes that cause you to regularly avoid certain events. Whether you're avoiding weddings, dates, or dentist appointments, having a better understanding of how your anxiety is affecting your life is important. Remember that putting this type of effort into improving your life is something you should feel proud of. Self-progression isn't easy but it can be wonderfully rewarding.

Overcoming your fears and changing your habits will take some time. Socializing may be intimidating to you now but if you want to get over it and move on with your life, you've got to start getting some practice. If you really want to make a change, be committed to yourself and your progress. Know and believe that you deserve more out of life. **Social anxiety is something that anyone can beat.** There is no overnight cure but there are plenty of things you can do to let go of anxiety for good. Here are four things you can start doing right now:

1 - Organize your thoughts.

When we're experiencing anxiety, our minds can run at about a thousand miles per hour. Racing thoughts are a common symptom of anxiety and they are almost always negative or catastrophic. When we're thinking about too many things at once, we can get flustered, experience panic attacks, and want nothing more than to flee the scene. In addition, a racing mind can cause exhaustion, headaches, an upset stomach, and difficulty concentrating. If social anxiety is causing your attention span to be compromised, it can be hard to follow conversations. You may be easily distracted by your increased heart rate, sweaty palms, or other things going on in the room.

To get a hold on your thoughts, try to pare it down and slow it down. Start by practicing this when you're feeling flustered or stressed out. Tell yourself that you are only going to think about one thing at a time and actively try to stay focused on that thing. For instance, if you're cleaning the house and you have a tendency to walk around doing a little bit of this and a little bit of that, pare it down by doing one thing at a time and really let yourself be present in that moment. Only allow yourself to think about that one thing and think it slowly.

Right now, I am doing the dishes and that is all I'm doing. Right now, I am brushing my teeth. If you tend to multitask on your computer, pare it down and slow it down. Don't check your email, refresh all your feeds, research the right kind of puppy to get, and try to do your taxes all at once. Just do one thing at a time and take it slowly. *Right now, I am ordering my groceries. Right now, I am doing my banking. Right now, I am checking my email.* In order to keep yourself from flitting from one thing to another, try closing down all other open windows and apps on your computer so that your attention is solely on one thing at a time.

This is a great way to lower your stress levels and become more productive. But the best part is that, the more you practice slowing things down and doing one thing at a time, the easier it will be to grab hold of your thoughts when they start to race. This way you'll have more control over your mind and you'll be less distracted by your anxiety.

Meditation is a wonderful way to practice mastery over your mind and I highly recommend giving it a try. But for now, just by actively thinking this way in your everyday life, you will gain the control you need to feel steady and comfortable when you're in a busy social setting. The aim is to be able to focus on a conversation or other social experience without becoming distracted. This means going to the movies and actually watching the movie rather than worrying about the next time you're going to have to get up to go to the bathroom. It means going to your children's piano recitals without worrying about bumping into someone you know. Being present in the moment means letting go of worry and fear. It means not thinking about what *could happen*, but rather, focusing on what *is happening*.

In addition, being able to slow things down both physically and mentally can be of great benefit in times that are particularly stressful or emotionally demanding. This means that if things at work are heating up, you'll be able to cope better with higher demands and keep your cool under pressure. So too, if you're going through something which is very emotionally taxing such as a bereavement or being diagnosed with a serious illness, being able to slow things down and take things one step at a time will keep things from spinning out of control. So remember, when it feels like things are starting to get on top of you, pare it down and slow it down.

2 - Conquer the Stop and Chat!

If you dread running into people you know on the street, you're not alone! Very few people enjoy those unexpected moments where you're on the bus and someone you know gets on and sits down beside you. Many of us keep our gaze down or try to look busy on our phones just to prevent it from happening! Some of us will go as far as to actively cross the street or change direction just to avoid running into someone we know! But when you break it down, being freaked out by a stop and chat is a pretty irrational fear. Yes, it's an unexpected meeting which means you haven't had time to prepare for it. Yes, you'll have to think on your feet. Yes, you might say something embarrassing. And yes, you might not remember the person's name or even where you know them from. So it's only natural that you might feel some anxiety where chance meetings are concerned.

But don't forget that the other person is probably having similar thoughts and feelings. And chances are, they will go away thinking about all the things they could've said better if they'd had time to prepare. Keep in mind as well, that the meeting will not go on forever, even if it feels never ending! Like most fears, facing the stop and chat is the quickest way to get over it. Challenge yourself to engage in an unplanned conversation the next time you run into someone unexpectedly (unless of course, one of you are in a rush). Remember that when you meet someone on the street, you're both going somewhere, so the conversation isn't going too last long unless you're walking in the same direction. And if you're running late, it's fine to say, "I'm sorry, I'm running late but it was good to see you."

However, if you're not running late, prove to yourself that you can endure the chance meeting. Start a conversation by asking questions. "Hey, how are things with you?" If you remember something this person was up to recently, ask them how it went. Say something like, "How was that exhibition last week? I would've loved to have been there." Ask about their partner or their kids. Ask them how work is. Focusing on asking questions and listening to the answers is actually a great way to make people like you. The number one rule of having a healthy conversation is *listen first, talk second*. This bodes well if your anxiety has your jaw clamped shut.

When the person reciprocates with questions about you, remember that you don't have to divulge everything that's going on in your life. In a stop and chat, it's more about politeness than catching up. It's fine to say, *"All good here. Nothing out of the ordinary!"* Or if you have some news, throw that out there. *"Actually, I just started a new job."* Remember to keep it light and steer clear of negatives if possible. Try not to open with, *"My dog just died, I'm behind on my rent, and I'm really, really tired."* Most importantly, remember to pare it down and slow it down. This conversation will probably only last for 1-3 minutes.

When it's time to end it, just say, *"well, I better get going. Good to see you!"* You can of course reference something they said like, *"Good luck with that job interview!"* or *"Hope that you and the kids enjoy your weekend away!"*. When it's over, walk away with your head held high and give yourself a pat on the back for conquering a fear. Don't dwell on any parts of the conversation that didn't really flow. Let yourself feel more confident and more settled in yourself. Know that the next time you run into someone on the street, you have the skills and confidence you need to engage in an unplanned conversation. There's nothing to be afraid of anymore.

3 - When you say you'll be there, BE THERE.

You are aware now that regularly canceling plans is a common compulsion for people living with social anxiety. If you know that you're the type of person who cancels plans a lot or you have a tendency to not show up when you say you'll be somewhere, you should have already taken some time to explore why this is. Now you can challenge yourself to think even deeper about it. Remember that anxiety is a personal experience. It differs from person to person and this is why understanding the nature of the beast is so important. Understanding how your anxiety affects *you* is the best way to gain power over it.

Start by identifying which types of social events you usually avoid by thinking about your canceling habit in a variety of contexts. Think about get togethers with your friends, family, and colleagues. Think about doctor appointments, job interviews, and large social gatherings. Are you fine with smaller, one-on-one meetings with friends but anxious at larger parties? Do all social gatherings seem daunting? Are you able to make and attend medical and/or business appointments?

Now think about *when* you usually decide to avoid these events and try to identify any patterns. Do you know right from the start that you're not going to attend? Do you decide to cancel a week before the event? A day before? An hour before? What thoughts and feelings are usually going through your mind when you decide to stay at home? Would you say that you know it's anxiety that's keeping you from going out or are you more likely focus on excuses like, *"I have nothing to wear"* or *"It's too cold outside, I'd rather stay in"*. Try to question yourself like this every time you see yourself canceling or avoiding events.

There are certain times when all of us feel anxious about going out. For instance, if you're likely to run into an ex or someone you don't get along with, it's only natural to feel apprehensive. This is a topic I will discuss at length later but for now, try to think beyond excuses and get to the root of the problem.

Do you stay in because your self-confidence is low? Are you nervous about making small talk? Being in the spotlight? Doing something embarrassing? Are you afraid of panic attacks or anxiety itself? Do you just prefer to stay at home? If so, why?

It's important to remember that insecurities are felt by everyone at one point or another. None of us have our heads held high *all* the time. And if you can't quite put your finger on why you feel so anxious or why you cancel plans so much, don't stress yourself out about it. Just try to revisit that topic occasionally, especially after an attack of anxiety. Sometimes what you have to overcome isn't necessarily a specific fear at all; it might just be a mental block or a tendency to self-sabotage. The important thing is to get into the habit of reflecting on your thoughts and feelings so that you can gain more knowledge and control over your anxiety. If chronic canceling is affecting your quality of life, it needs to be eradicated. This is about you and your life. You don't get to do it all over again. When it's over, it's over, so try to make the best of it.

If you're really not sure what's causing you to cancel plans or all of the ideas above seem to hit home, consider the possibility that canceling has simply become a bad habit. Habits are hard to break and the more we avoid things, the bigger they seem in our heads. Try breaking your habit by listing 5 or 10 events that you regularly cancel or avoid. Rate them based on how anxious they make you feel, with 1 being the easiest to attend and 10 being the hardest. Tackle your list starting with the 1's, and then move onto the bigger challenges. Each time you attend an event, reflect on how it made you feel. Most importantly, give yourself credit for overcoming that hurdle every time you do it. Recognize that you are making a positive change in your life. Treat yourself to something special and remember that with every hurdle, you are getting stronger.

4 - Let Go and Lighten Up!

Being able to let go is the ultimate freedom. Allowing yourself to take things lightly and free yourself from obsessive and harmful thinking is a skill that all of us need. Life is fleeting and being able to embrace that reality won't just give you perspective; it will also help you let go of your worries, forgive your embarrassments, and release your regrets. This means that you can live in the present without being bogged down by past baggage and future worries. Accept that you cannot change things that have already happened. You cannot alter what you've said in any given moment.

Rerunning that bad experience or that uncomfortable conversation over and over in your head will not change it, nor will it make you feel any better about it. There comes a point when you simply have to let it go. For your own sanity, your own feelings of self worth, and your potential for healthy and enjoyable social interactions in the future, let yourself be light. Let go of whatever is holding you down.

Case Study: James

James was an extreme case; a chronic "no-show". For years, he had been accepting invitations to parties and promising he'd be there, but he never actually went anywhere. At the time, he just preferred to spend his spare time at home and he didn't want to disappoint his friends by saying he wouldn't be able to attend. That's what he told himself anyway, but the longer it went on, the less he wanted to socialize at all. In the early years, he didn't recognize that he even had social anxiety, he just thought of himself as an introvert. A lone wolf.

After a number of years went by, his canceling and avoidance spread to other parts of his life. Work events that were avoidable, were avoided. Doctor appointments went from being mandatory to optional. Things he used to enjoy doing like playing sports and taking his dog Max to the beach were off the list too. James looks back at these times and remembers specifically when things were so bad that when his mother would call him on the phone, he wouldn't answer. They'd had a very close relationship throughout his life but his avoidance had become bigger than him. No matter who it was that was calling, he just couldn't seem to make himself answer the phone. So he got used to just letting it ring out. At least this way he wouldn't have to tell his mum that he wouldn't be visiting anytime soon. He told himself that was a good thing.

At its worst, James's social anxiety made it hard for him to even do his own shopping. He ordered everything online. Going to the grocery store gave him panic attacks. At work he was demoted, and eventually he got another job working from home. It was a lonely existence but he was in so deep it was hard to see a way out.

I first started talking to James after his mother had passed away. He was guilt ridden for having rarely visited her in her last few years. And on top of that, her death had reminded him that life would end for him one day too. I still can't believe how quickly James overcame his social anxiety. He knew that he had to do something to grab hold of the reins. He was so determined, so dedicated to making his life happier and healthier, that in just a matter of months, he was a different person. He'd been lost in the darker side of life but he found his way back. He got back into playing sports and started taking Max on big days out again. And with the positive change all that exercise had on his physique, he got the confidence to start socializing again. I truly believe that if someone like James can overcome avoidance and anxiety, anyone can.

Panic Attacks No More

A considerable amount of people with social anxiety also suffer from panic attacks. And if you are one of them, you'll know that panic can make everything in life more difficult. Socializing can be unbelievably daunting if you're always worried about being hit with an attack. Virtually anything can trigger panic; it can come out of nowhere. So let me start this section with a few facts. First, panic attacks are real. These crippling and debilitating attacks of anxiety often get stuffed in that condescending category of things that are "only in your head"; however, the emotional experience and physical effects of panic attacks are very real indeed. Second, panic attacks are common.

Around 1 in 10 people will experience them at some point in their lives, a small portion of which will have recurring attacks lasting anywhere from days to years. Third, panic attacks are not physically dangerous. I like to stress the word "physically" because I believe that on an emotional and mental level, recurring panic attacks can cause heightened levels of fear and stress as well as skewing the lines of reality to some extent.

If you experience panic attacks and you're living with social anxiety, life can seem pretty grim at times. Going out and socializing can be hard enough without the added possibility of a panic episode. But your panic does not have to stay with you for the rest of your life. If you want to make it go away, you can.

Let's start by getting to know the nature of the beast! Panic attacks are truly nasty things. Although attacks originate in your thoughts (whether conscious or unconscious), they can cause sudden and dramatic physical changes that can be downright terrifying. Heart palpitations, sweaty palms, shortness of breath, tingling hands and face, blurred vision, feelings of impending doom or fear of losing control… none of these things are pleasant and all of them could lead you to think that you're having a seizure, stroke, or heart attack. But believing something terrible is happening doesn't mean that you've lost your mind. Most of these catastrophic thoughts are rooted in some very real processes your body is going through, almost all of which are caused by a serge of adrenaline.

When we're in danger, our bodies release extra adrenaline to help us get away or fight. This is known as the *fight or flight* response. Adrenaline can have a number of worrying effects on the physical body. It can increase your blood pressure and cause your blood vessels contract, thus redirecting your blood flow toward your heart and lungs. So that rapidly pounding heart that you experience when you're panicking is not a figment of your imagination. It's a real physical process.

Furthermore, adrenaline opens your airways so as to get more oxygen into your muscles. So while your breathing continues gets faster, the extra oxygen coursing through your body might make you hyperventilate, feel lightheaded or dizzy, and experience tingling in your hands, feet, or face. Adrenaline also causes a heightened sense of awareness so that if you're being pursued by a predator, you will be more able to perceive danger and escape more easily. Hence, when you're panicking, your senses are working at their maximum capacity, so it makes sense that lights may seem too bright and sounds might be deafeningly loud. These bodily changes can last around an hour or more and may leave you feeling restless, irritable, exhausted, or unable to sleep. And these are just the physical effects!

What happens in our minds is a little more complex and will naturally vary from person to person. Most of us will become intensely focused on what's happening to our body. We become afraid that we might be dying or experiencing a serious physical ailment. We may develop behavioral patterns such as checking our pulse repeatedly, touching our face and hair a lot, checking to see if our hands are shaking, drinking a lot of water, and obsessively scanning our body for changes. We might need to sit down or we may prefer fleeing the situation that brought the panic on. Some of us will feel bewildered and taken off guard by an attack. Others who experience attacks more regularly, might be able to predict them and therefore purposefully avoid situations that they find panic inducing.

In a way, the nature of panic attacks could be considered fascinating. Our bodies have this built in fight or flight response but sometimes the system is faulty. This is why some people kick into fight or flight by simply getting on the bus. Others might experience it when a loved one is ill. Some people hate elevators; others get panic attacks when their stress levels are particularly high. The possibilities are endless and entirely personal. But if our mind decides to kick into fight or flight mode when there's no true danger, what can we do to turn it off? The answer is, we need to use our conscious mind - our ability to reason and think logically - to talk our unconscious mind off the cliff. We need to keep our cool.

If you experience panic attacks regularly, you might feel constantly on edge waiting for the next attack. This could mean that you avoid any situation that might bring one on; the most obvious trigger (for the purpose of this book) being socializing. If you get panic attacks from the same stimuli often enough, in a way, you have an advantage. Yes, always having panic attacks at the grocery store doesn't exactly make you feel like you're on top of the world but, if you've survived the situation before, you will be more able to look at the evidence and view the situation logically which is exactly what you need to do to get panic under control.

But no matter who you are and whether this is your first panic attack or your hundredth attack, you have the power to break the situation down to basics and use your logical mind to get you through it. Here are some examples to illustrate what I mean.

Example #1: Let's say that riding the bus is the thing that causes your attacks. You get on the bus, your anxiety starts to rise, fight or flight mode kicks in and your body is flooded with adrenaline. The physical effects of the adrenaline are making you believe that you're going to die or have a stroke. What's happening physically is severely unpleasant but even if you feel powerless, being able to think logically will give you the upper hand. Ask yourself some questions to realistically assess the danger and get a logical hold on the situation.

Ask yourself: What evidence do you have to prove that you are not dying nor having a seizure or stroke?

Answer: I have experienced this before. I've been on the bus and felt like this in the past, and I did not die nor did I have a stroke or seizure. Therefore, what I am having is a panic attack. It is not dangerous and I am not going to die on this bus.

Ask yourself: What is the worst thing that could happen on this journey?

Answer: I could throw up or pass out. I might cause a scene or have to get off the bus before my stop.

Ask yourself: Have you ever thrown up, passed out, or caused a scene on the bus before?

Answer: No.

Ask yourself: How would people react if you did get sick or pass out?

Answer: They'd probably be concerned for me and offer me help.

Ask yourself: What happens if you get off the bus before your stop?

Answer: I'll have to walk a bit further.

Of course these questions and answers will vary from person to person but getting used to thinking this way is a powerful way to talk yourself down when panic is trying to win you over. It may seem a bit tedious at first but soon it will become second nature. Remember that having panic attacks in certain situations now, does not mean that you will be stuck with them for the rest of your life. You just have to get control of your mind and fix that faulty fight or flight system. You have to be able to think logically and realistically in order to retrain the response you have to your particular triggers.

Example 2: You believe that you have to sit near an exit at all times but when you arrive late to a work meeting, you find that all the seats are taken except for the one farthest from the door. Fight or flight mode kicks in and now, on top of thinking you might die or throw up, you're also afraid that you won't be able to concentrate on what's happening in the meeting. And what if they want you to speak? What if you have to go to the bathroom?!

Ask yourself: What is the worst thing that could happen in this room?
Answer: I might have to excuse myself to go to the bathroom. I might say something stupid. Or I might be so panicky that I won't hear if someone asks me a question.

Ask yourself: And then what?
Answer: I'll just go to the bathroom, clarify what I meant to say, or I'll ask them to repeat the question.

Ask yourself: Will you survive that?
Answer: Yes, but it would be better if I was sitting by the door.

Ask yourself: Why do you think you have to sit by the door?
Answer: Because I don't like feeling trapped.

Ask yourself: Are you trapped? Are you tied to the chair? Could you get up and walk out if you needed to?
Answer: No, I'm not actually trapped. I can get up and leave anytime I want. But I wouldn't want to cause a scene by walking out of the room.

Ask yourself: Have you ever accused someone of making a scene when they've left a room to use the bathroom?
Answer: No, that's ridiculous.

Ask yourself: What will people think if you get up and leave at any point during the meeting?
Answer: They'll probably just think I had to go to the bathroom.

Ask yourself: Will that be a catastrophe? Will you lose your job because you had to go to the bathroom?
Answer: No.

Asking yourself questions this way not only distracts you from your irrational fears but it also helps you slow down your thinking and get some logical perspective on the situation at hand. Remember, regardless of what your body is trying to tell you, you are not in danger. This is all nothing but smoke and mirrors. You *can* beat this.

There are plenty of other things you can do to reduce the amount of attacks you have and lessen the severity of them. First, try reminding yourself that no matter what event you are attending, it WILL end eventually. You won't be on that bus forever. Your work meeting will end before the day is over. A wedding ceremony, a date, a night out, a flight to visit your in-laws, all of these things are temporary. You are not trapped, there is nothing to worry about. Keep that mind when you're in situations that usually ramp up your anxiety. Just try to give in to the situation at hand. Resign yourself to being there. Try not to *fight* it or obsess over it.

Strip it down to basics and allow yourself to just be present in the moment. *Right now, I'm on an airplane. Right now I'm at a party. Right now I'm in a meeting. There is no danger here and I won't be here forever.* Remember that you are allowed to actually have fun when you're out! Once you're strong enough to ditch the anxiety and embrace the positive aspects of socializing, you're likely to find that your life is a lot lighter and more enjoyable. We need other people in our lives; there is no reason to deny ourselves of that vital necessity.

It is important to note, that the vast majority of times you're panicking, other people can't see it. They don't know what you're thinking or feeling. Your anxiety is almost always invisible to them. But if you can fake feeling cool, calm, and collected for a few minutes, you might actually start to feel better. There is some truth in the phrase "fake it till you make it". The more we smile, the happier we will actually become. Likewise, the more we frown, the worse we're likely to feel. So why not pretend to be having a good time for a while? You've got nothing to lose.

Furthermore, if other people can't see your panic attacks, remember that you probably can't see theirs either. If you're in a room with a hundred people in it, theoretically there could be ten people panicking at the same time. Try looking around the next time you're in a room full of people and guess who's having a hard time being there. Chances are, you won't be able to tell, but you'll know that you're not alone.

Remember, the fears behind your panic attacks may be irrational and nonsensical but you are not stupid or weird for having them. You're not crazy, and you're not a failure. Panic attacks can happen to anyone. They're not just for people who are "weak" or "sad" or "mentally ill". Panic doesn't discriminate, and once it has a hold on you, it can be a dominating force in your life. One of the most common and most difficult facets of panic is that once you've had an attack, you're likely to develop a fear of panic itself. This could mean that when it comes to social gatherings, you might not be afraid of socializing at all. Rather, it is possible that it's the fear of having a panic attack *while* you're socializing that's actually causing your anxiety.

So too, if you get panic attacks on buses, it's probably not simply the act of getting on the bus that you're actually afraid of. On a rational level, taking the bus doesn't really put you at risk for many major disasters. So it's possible that the thing you're really afraid of, is *panicking* on the bus. Ask yourself now: Is the thing that triggers your attacks what you're really afraid of? Or is it the panic attacks themselves that are dominating your social life? If panic attacks are stealing your life from you, practice looking at the evidence and thinking slowly and logically. Once you gain control over panic attacks, the world will seem a much friendlier place.

It can be helpful to tell someone you trust about your panic attacks as well so that you have some extra support. This is especially helpful if you're attending an event with that person and you're worried that you might have an attack while you're there. Often just saying that you *might* have a panic attack is enough to keep it from happening. Sometimes all we need in order to get some temporary freedom from a fear is to simply say it out loud. Plus if someone knows about your worries, you can tell them if panic does arise and they might be able help talk you down. If you are going to lean on a friend for help, tell them a few things that you know will help you so that they can get fully on board. Be sure to tell someone whom you know will be sensitive with you. Telling a friend or family member who's likely to ridicule or disrespect you will probably not be of any assistance.

Finally, although panic attacks can be extremely unpleasant, exposing yourself to your triggers a little at a time will help you build a tolerance to them. If you can only stay on the bus long enough to go one stop away, that's fine! If you can only do one lap around the grocery store, that's better than nothing. But when you do take those small steps, tell yourself that you've conquered some of that fear and let it go. You are now free to take the bus from one stop to another. You can now endure the grocery store for five or six minutes. Next time, go two stops. Do two laps of the store. Then, three stops. Three laps… You get the gist.

Remember to give yourself credit for these small feats. They are significant proof of the commitment you've made to your self-progression. Don't put yourself down because other people might not have the same obstacles as you. Let yourself feel good!

Case Study: Anthony

Anthony suffered from panic attacks to a terrible degree. He'd started having them when he was in college, likely because of the pressure he was under to work full time and do well in school despite his exhaustion. But after a number of years, he was so used to his attacks that he rarely even had to think about them. He had structured his whole life around them. When he'd graduated college, he got a job working from home. Luckily Anthony had met his wife, Helen, long before he'd developed social anxiety and she was happy to work around his panic attacks. So rather than encouraging him to overcome panic, she joined him in avoiding his triggers.

But avoiding things that would cause an attack didn't mean that Anthony was cured. Rather, the older he got, he developed more and more anxiety provokers. He still suffered from attacks when he was forced to leave the house, and as the years went by, things between he and Helen became strained.

When his wife threatened to leave him, Anthony put himself through an intense program to gradually overcome his triggers. He wasn't going to choose anxiety over his wife. So little by little, he began going places that would normally trigger his attacks. He encouraged himself to stay in each situation until his panic died down, rather than fleeing right away. He gradually increased the amount of time he could endure being in these situations without anxiety getting the better of him. He made fantastic progress and Helen was beyond proud of him.

But the real test was when Anthony got free tickets to a comedy show. He couldn't think of a more panic inducing setting and so, feeling determined to prove himself he agreed to take Helen to the show and vowed to give her a great night out. When they arrived at the venue they realized that their seats were in the middle of the front row. Anthony got a sinking feeling in his stomach. Sitting in those seats at a comedy show was a pretty risky ordeal. He knew that he and Helen were likely to get picked on by the comedian at some point in the show. Sweat beaded on his forehead and his hands started to shake. Noticing his hesitation, Helen encouraged him to just stand still and breathe for a while until his anxiety passed. She had seen him freeze up like this many times before and didn't want to forfeit their night out just because their seats weren't near an exit. When his anxiety dropped down to mild irritation, they took their seats.

Anthony felt like he was starting to relax a little but as soon as the show began, the comedian began pouncing on the audience. He started with the people just to the left of them, and then moved to the people on their right. Anthony barely heard a single joke over the beating of his own heart. "Please don't pick us... please don't pick us..."

At intermission, Anthony asked Helen if maybe she'd like to go home. They'd lucked out by having not been picked on so far, and they should probably just cut their losses and go home before the *comedian turned his attention to them. Helen refused. She was having a good time and she was sick of his anxiety getting in the way of their fun. "Just try to let go and enjoy yourself... Try to let yourself be light. Remember not to take things too seriously. We're just having a fun night out." Reluctantly, Anthony agreed. He didn't want to let her down. He didn't want to ruin another night for her. So they went back in and took their seats.*

As soon as the comedian came back on stage he turned his attention to them. Anthony froze as the spotlight landed on him and Helen. He felt the color drain from his face. He was in such a state of nervousness that he could barely hear anything the comedian was saying. But soon, he was forced to engage with the show; forced to speak in front of a crowd! To his surprise, after a minute or so, Anthony was laughing. He was actually having fun. He was still nervous but he knew that anyone would be nervous in that setting. And luckily for Helen, he was able to maintain that perspective for the duration of the show.

When it was all over, Anthony was buzzing. He and Helen had finally had the great night out that they'd never been able to have before. He felt proud of himself. He'd faced his fears! And by staying put and engaging with the people around him, by letting himself be light and keeping his cool, he'd kept his panic at bay and replaced it with happiness and celebration.

Giving Harmful Behavior The Boot

Human beings are creatures of habit. We do our best work when we're in a healthy routine and when we take good care of our bodies and minds. Having good habits can mean that our mood is likely to be lighter and more positive overall. And when these things are good, the ways in which we relate to others may be more natural, compassionate, and understanding. But if we develop bad habits along the way, all of our hard work can be reduced to nil. If you're feeling low, it's natural to become defensive or withdrawn from others; it's easy to let the tides of depression and self-doubt overcomes you. We all struggle with bad habits and harmful behavior in life, even when we don't recognize it. Eating unhealthy foods, staying up too late at night, sabotaging your relationships, showing up late to work, remaining in abusive or manipulative friendships, all of these things are common pitfalls of adulthood. But if you're stuck in a rut and you know your life needs a bit of an overhaul, you might want to think about ditching your bad habits for good. If you do so, you'll probably find that your experiences with social anxiety will lessen.

Following on from the previous section, let's take another look at panic attacks. Let's start by looking at some harmful habits that might be inviting your panic attacks to hang around a little while longer than you'd like them to. When we experience recurring panic attacks, it's natural for us to develop certain *safety behaviors* in the hopes of keeping panic at bay.

Here are a few examples:
Insisting on sitting near an exit or bathroom at all times
Avoiding sitting too close to other people, especially in smaller spaces
Avoiding sitting in the middle of a row at the movie theater or in similar places at other seated events
Insisting on having water to hand at all times
Making repeated trips to the bathroom
Obsessively rehearsing an escape route "just in case"
Frequently checking the time or counting down the minutes you'll have to spend at an event
Frequently checking your phone or pretending to be texting when you're not
Attempting to distract yourself with a game or familiar thought process
Obsessively scanning your body for any changes in your physical state

A lot of these behaviors may seem completely harmless but to someone who suffers from panic attacks, these habits could mean the difference between getting over your attacks and being stuck with them for life. It might be hard to believe but *safety* behaviors can be pretty dangerous. I have mentioned before that the more you avoid something, the harder it will be to face it. In this case, the more you *do* something, the harder it is to *stop* doing it.

For example, if you insist on sitting by the door every time you enter a room, you're likely to feel an increase to your anxiety when that seat is unavailable. Sitting by the door all the time is actively, and repeatedly, telling yourself that the rest of the room is unsafe. You are effectively, reiterating the exact same thing your panic is telling you; hence, giving an irrational fear even more power over you. This habit isn't making you *safe* at all. It's making you even more prone to anxiety and panic attacks.

Have you ever noticed that if you take your pulse when you starting to panic, it actually gets faster the whole time you're counting? Have you ever thought that the reason it might do that is because the more you focus on bodily changes, the more your anxiety rises? The more you scan your body for subtle changes, the more freaked out you're going to be when they occur; hence, even more adrenaline gets pumped into your system and the symptoms of panic increase. It's a vicious cycle. But if you actively choose *not* to scan your body - if you don't take your pulse, you don't take your temperature or check for jittery hands - the symptoms of increased adrenaline, will ease off a lot more quickly. Panic is a very attention seeking entity. If you give it your attention, it acts up. If you rationalize it and don't give it the attention it desires, it subsides. The same can be said for social anxiety.

Have another look at that list of safety behaviors above and try to apply this theory to each of them. Does constantly having a water bottle really make you feel less nervous? Has having water with you all this time cured your panic attacks? Or is it possible that carrying that water bottle is making you believe that you need it; making you think there is real danger nearby; making you invite panic? If you sit in the middle of a row at the theater, are you really trapped there?

Surely you have the freedom to get up and leave anytime you want. People get up to use the bathroom during movies all the time! Since you stopped sitting in the middle of rows, have your panic attacks and anxiety disappeared? Have the stayed the same or increased? Ask yourself: Are the things you're afraid of rational or irrational? If they are irrational, are your safety behaviors really helping you get rid of your anxiety or are they just helping you hold onto it?

Over the next few days or weeks, try to identify what your safety behaviors are and start challenging them. Letting go of these habits is not easy by any means. A lot of these behaviors will be things you've been doing for years in the belief that they were helping you keep your cool. But if you still have panic attacks and anxiety, it's probably time to try something different. Yes, it's going to be scary. Yes, it's going to be difficult. Yes, it will probably be emotionally activating. But if ditching a few bad habits means freeing yourself from anxiety, it's worth a try.

Just remember to take things slowly. This isn't going to be an overnight cure. You might have a better understanding of your anxiety and safety behaviors now, but they will probably be things you'll need to chip away at over time. Start small. Try going somewhere without your water bottle. You can keep it in the car or have a friend hold it for you while you navigate some time and space without it. Wherever you are and whatever habit you're trying to break, try to stay in the situation until your fear dies down rather than reaching for your safety behavior at the very start. Let yourself experience the fear and then let it fade away. Over time, as and when you feel ready, gradually increase your exposure to life without safety behaviors.

I have mentioned the danger of avoidance a few times so far, but apart from simply not going out, there are quite a few other ways avoidance can creep into your life. Remember, social anxiety doesn't just live at parties and on dates. It can be a much bigger, much more *dominating*, force than that.

Here are a few other types of avoidance for you to think about:
Inviting people to come to your house rather than going out
Leaving an event early, often before you've had a chance to settle

Wearing headphones or keeping your head down while walking or taking public transport in case you run into someone you know

Convincing yourself that no one actually wants you to come out anyway

Making sure that you're always the first person there so that you don't have to awkwardly look around for your friends

Making sure that you're always the last person there so no one notices your arrival

Not going anywhere alone

Not applying for jobs or promotions because you're too nervous to speak to people of authority

Making excuses to not go out, such as not wanting to spend too much money or having nothing to wear

Making yourself busy with other things

Not committing to attending an event so that you can get out of it easily

Making phone calls or texting when you're at a social event, as if to keep one foot in the door and one foot out

Coming and going a lot i.e. for bathroom or smoke breaks

Avoidance is complex in that it's not quite as black and white as we may think. And when it comes to social anxiety, it can be a very dangerous habit. Avoidance behaviors are a lot like safety behaviors in that they are actively confirming your irrational fears. The more you indulge in them, the more intense your anxiety will grow. Avoidance can really hold us back in life; it can mean losing out on social bonds and altering the way we feel about ourselves. If we're always avoiding things that we find challenging or things that push us outside our comfort zone, how is that likely to affect our self-esteem?

What self-beliefs might we develop as a result? We might think of ourselves as cowardly or easily intimidated. We might believe that we *can't* do things that we actually *can* do. We might feel "different" from other people, not good enough, or destined to have less in life. If self-beliefs like these are allowed to creep into our thoughts, social anxiety is likely to maintain its hold on us for even longer.

Over the next day or two, be on the look out for ways avoidance might be affecting you and write them down. Every time you see yourself shying away from something challenging or altering your plans so that they'll work better with your anxiety, make a note of it. Don't worry about analyzing these things if you're busy or distracted at the time. But when you have some time on your hands, reflect on your avoidance and think about what's driving it. Think about how avoidance is affecting you and your relationships and make some attempts at counteracting it. Instead of inviting a friend to come to your house, suggest going to theirs. Instead of making excuses to stay in for the night, fess up to the real reasons you don't want to go out and challenge those self-imposed limitations. You might not feel able to go out to a big party right away but simply attempting to understand your avoidance is a step in the right direction. Remember to be kind to yourself throughout this process. No one gets better by putting themselves down. Social anxiety is not a weakness; it's just an obstacle you happen to be battling right now. Treat yourself kindly and lift yourself up. Just treat yourself the same way you'd treat a friend in the same situation. Be patient with yourself.

Case Study: Jessica

Jessica was once a master of avoidance. She had been an introvert her whole life and although she had plenty of friends, she rarely met up with them anywhere other than at her own house. The only time she would agree to go out is if her friends agreed to meet somewhere that was small and quiet. Having to raise her voice over noisy crowds made her feel uncomfortable, and seeing how other people seemed to find socializing so easy always made her feel bad about herself.

At work, Jessica had one or two people that she spoke to from time to time, but mostly she kept to herself. When her colleagues went out for drinks after work, she never went with them, despite the fact that they invited her every time. She preferred only seeing them in the confinements of work where everyone had a job to do and her encounters with others were predictable to some extent. Throughout the two decades she spent working for the same company, Jessica had never applied for a promotion or asked for a raise. Opportunities came and went and even though she knew she was more than qualified to advance in the company, she stayed put in her position. She didn't feel the need to boast about herself and her capabilities. She didn't want to have to talk about herself in an interview or meeting. She found things a lot easier when she didn't get too much attention.

Jessica's avoidance kept her deeply rooted in her comfort zone. She didn't feel confident enough to try new things and she was nervous about having to navigate social encounters. She'd never been a social butterfly so she hadn't had a lot of practice where socializing was concerned. She was addicted to predictability. She was at her most comfortable when she knew what to expect. The idea of talking to people without a plan or pre-rehearsed script made her nervous and uncomfortable. She was happy with things the way they were.

But as the years passed, Jessica's happiness waned. She felt isolated and lonely. She didn't like the fact that on social media, everyone else's lives seemed to be so much more fun than hers. She was stagnant and her comfort zone was starting to feel more like a trap. She knew that it was time for a change; being an introvert didn't have to mean being miserable or leading a boring life. She wanted more than that.

For Jessica, conquering avoidance was not an easy process. Her social habits were so deeply ingrained that she didn't even know they were there. She had to start by thinking about the ways in which she was holding herself back. She needed to reflect on why she made the decisions she did. Why hadn't she advanced with her career? Why was she so isolated? Why did she always say no when she was invited out? What could she change about her behavior that would get her out of her life long rut?

Jessica's saboteur was her comfort zone. In order to be the person she wanted to be and get the life she wanted to have, she had to push herself out of those confinements. So each week, Jessica set herself a task. She didn't allow herself to make excuses and she didn't let social anxiety steal her life away from her anymore. One week she *met a friend out in a busy venue. She only stayed for an hour but it was longer than she'd ever stayed in an environment like that in the past. She knew that just setting foot in that place was a big step. The next week, she attended a small party at a relative's house. She engaged in conversation even though she couldn't predict what people were going to say. It was actually a lot easier than she'd thought it would be. People were warm and inviting and she actually enjoyed herself! Eventually, she accepted the invitation to go out with the crew from work.*

The more she reached out of that comfort zone, the better she was starting to feel about herself. She was getting stronger while her social anxiety was getting weaker. She knew that as an introvert, she was never going to be the loudest or most outspoken person in the room, but that didn't mean that she wasn't fun to be around. She had a lot to offer and if she hadn't have pushed herself out of the confinements of her old predictable life, she may have never known what life was like on the outside.

Jessica's life now bears little resemblance to what it was like in the past. She goes out at least once a week now and has recently started dating. She finally applied for that promotion and got it. She is open to new things now and she feels like life is full of possibilities.

Learning to recognize when our thoughts or actions are holding us back is vitally important to getting beyond our personal obstacles in life. We all have different struggles and different quirks. We all have different pasts and different physiological make-ups. We must learn to be patient with ourselves as well as being persistent about the things we'd like to change.

Before going on to the next section, I am going to briefly cover another handful of harmful habits to be on the look out for. These are things that may be holding you back, making you feel bad about yourself, or even dictating how you think about life overall. Try not to fly through this section too quickly. Rather, take some time to think on these things and try to identify any bad habits that might be relevant to you in your life. Take good care of yourself throughout this process. What you are doing takes bravery and dedication and you deserve credit for that.

Bad Habits & How To Banish Them

1 - Indulging in "reruns" of embarrassing or shameful moments

Many times, social anxiety is rooted in a fear of embarrassment, shame, or generally considering yourself to be subpar among your peers. It can be hard not to compare yourself to others, and even harder to not feel down about things they've accomplished and you haven't. But these lines of thinking can be very harmful. They can lead to dwelling on negative past experiences and using those experiences to hold yourself back from taking risks and truly enjoying life. Sometimes it seems as if our embarrassing moments from the past are haunting us. They can be like ghosts from the past, popping up when we're feeling low, and making us feel even worse. Indulging in reruns of your less graceful moments can cause you to feel that embarrassment, shame, and insecurity all over again. If we insist on reliving our worst moments time and time again, it's no wonder we're afraid to get out and face more potential social follies.

We all feel embarrassed at times. We all say stupid things and act in ways we wish we hadn't. Overcoming embarrassment isn't easy, especially for people living with depression, low self-esteem, or social anxiety. Those past experiences can become a weapon for you to use against yourself. This is an ugly and painful cycle to get trapped in. If we all had to face every blunder and faux pas we've made throughout our lives on a daily basis, surely we'd all struggle with chronic embarrassment and feelings of low self worth.

The fact is, we're only human. We all make mistakes. None of us say the right thing all the time. None of us go through life without feeling embarrassed. But if we insist on holding onto the past - if we cling to our worst moments and let them dictate how we feel about ourselves - how will we ever be able to face life in the present? How can we possibly feel good about who we are if we won't forgive ourselves for our past mistakes? And how on earth can we face socializing if those embarrassing reruns keep playing over and over in our minds?

It's important to keep in mind that your embarrassing moments live in the *past*. There is nothing you can do to change them. You have to learn how to forgive yourself. You have to let your past experiences go. You have to be able to laugh at them. So you did something or said something embarrassing, so what? Who hasn't? Living in the present and feeling hopeful about the future isn't possible if we insist on clinging to the past. Let go of those things you torture yourself with. Let go of the fear that you might say something stupid again. The fact is, you probably will. Because we all will! This is a risk we take with face-to-face socializing; but it's a risk worth taking.

2 - Rehearsing upcoming conversations

For people with social anxiety, especially those who struggle with conversation in particular, it's common to get into the habit of rehearsing your upcoming conversations. This is especially true when it comes to things like job interviews or work meetings. However, there are some people whose lives are completely dominated by this compulsion. They'll rehearse telephone conversations, things they might say at a coffee date with a friend, difficult conversations regarding conflict resolution, how they'll ask a store attendant to help them find something, and virtually anything else. They might rehearse a conversation for days. They might be kept awake at night because that future conversation is relentlessly going around and around in their head. To me, it sounds like torture.

Don't get me wrong; there is absolutely nothing wrong with being prepared. Planning for a job interview, for example, is a pretty great idea, as long as you leave room for the possibility that you might get thrown a curve ball. If you over prepare and focus on things that are too specific, what happens when you get asked something you haven't prepared for? You might clam up, or you might try to use one of your pre-rehearsed answers even though it doesn't quite fit. You might end up losing your confidence or starting to panic. You might not get that job in the end.

Similarly, if you're on a date and you've prepared a bunch of things to talk about, how will you cope with a change of subject? And what will your date think about listening to your over rehearsed monologues? How might they feel when they realize that you aren't actually having a conversation with them, you're basically just reading from a teleprompter? Nothing about that will make them feel at ease.

Being over rehearsed can also make you talk faster than normally would. So too, being nervous might make you chatter away at light speed. If you know that nervousness makes you talk too fast, focus on breathing and speaking slowly. Talking slowly not only makes you appear less nervous, but it also gives you time to breathe naturally, and it gives the person you're talking to time to take in what you're saying. Conversation is a marathon, not a sprint.

So how do you prepare for social situations without rehearsing day and night? It's always good to have a few things you might like to talk about in mind but the real skill you need to be a good conversationalist is being a good listener. If you focus on listening rather than talking, you're making your conversational partner feel interesting and valued. Plus, by listening and truly engaging with what they're saying, you will find that your natural, unrehearsed answers are going to be just fine.

By asking someone questions about their life, rather than reciting a speech about yours, you're much more likely to be remembered in a positive light. Talking to people should be more about *relating* to them than it is about trying to *impress* them. And, by placing the focus on the person you're talking to, you will have a much easier time settling in and getting comfortable in that social sphere. By the time they ask questions about you, you should be feeling more relaxed.

The most important thing is to listen to the questions you're asked. If you're at a job interview, listen to what they're asking you before reciting what you've practiced. In any social environment, if you're not sure what someone is asking you, just ask them to clarify. Don't try to fudge your way through a conversation if you're not sure what it's really about! Remember that it's okay to plan to a certain extent but don't drive yourself crazy about what you're going to talk about for days leading up to an event. All that will do is place more pressure and importance on the event than is necessary.

Remember that these moments in our social lives are fleeting. No one will remember everything you've said. All of this is just a moment in time. Try not to put too much emphasis on it. Let yourself be light and just try to have fun!

3 - Beating yourself up and being too hard on yourself

This is one of the most dangerous habits human beings can succumb to. Throughout our lives there is only one thing that will be with us from the cradle to the grave, and that is *ourselves*. It is our responsibility to take care of number one. No one else is responsible for keeping us happy and healthy. People will come in and out of our lives and they will have positive and negative effects on us, but how we truly view ourselves, comes from within. If we don't care for ourselves, if we don't learn to love and accept ourselves, our lives will never be as good as they could be.

Learning to love yourself isn't always as easy as we'd like it to be. If you're too hard on yourself, you could easily get into the habit of beating yourself up every time you make a mistake. You might ridicule yourself for the way you look or for being single after everyone else has paired up. You might be angry with yourself for not being as successful as your peers or for struggling with anxiety when it seems like no one else does.

But beating yourself up is not a productive way to get anywhere in life. How can you possibly love yourself if you keep putting yourself down? How can you appreciate yourself for who you are if you're always focused on your failures? And how are you going to overcome social anxiety if think so poorly of yourself?

When it comes to taking care of number one, you have to be your own best friend, *not* your worst enemy. If you do put yourself down a lot, or if you tend to focus on your shortcomings too much, you've got to break that habit. Try treating yourself like a friend. Imagine that someone you care about is sitting in front of you, putting themselves down. How would you react to that? Would you agree with them? Would you say, "Yeah, I see what you're saying. You are a pretty terrible person. A real failure!" No. Of course you wouldn't. You would console them. You might offer them a hug and tell them all the reasons you think they're great.

If a friend was dwelling on something stupid they said, you would forgive them and encourage them to forgive themselves. You wouldn't spend your time being hard on your best friend, so why do it to yourself? You are the one person you're going to have to live with forever; it's time to come to grips with that and start giving yourself a break.

We all must accept that we are not perfect beings, but who we are is eternally special. The one thing that ties all human beings together is the fact that each one of us is unique. There have never been two people in the world that were exactly alike. No one has ever looked exactly like you, no one has had the same quirks, the same outlook on life, or the same talents. All of us are different and that's what makes us human. Isn't this something we should celebrate? You are who you are.

We all have room to grow, but we're lucky that we have the opportunity to continue to focus on self-progression and making our lives more enjoyable for as long as we live. When you're trying to overcome social anxiety, the last thing you need is to be emotionally sadistic toward yourself. Learning to lift yourself up means that you won't have to rely on others to do that for you.

4 - Self Sabotage

Self-sabotage comes in many forms. It can relate to how we interact with others, how we perform at work, and what our social life is like. Although it may come in many different shapes and sizes, one thing about self-sabotage is always true: It hurts you. The weird thing about this harmful habit is that it's not usually something that happens consciously. In fact, many times we don't know we're doing it at all. I think of self-sabotage as doing something to prevent your own potential happiness and success in life. And like anxiety, our reasons for sabotage are usually rooted in fear; most often, a fear of failure.

For instance, if someone has a habit of sabotaging their intimate relationships, they might rush the relationship to its end rather than being able to enjoy it and letting it run its natural course. They might do this by being unreliable, being cynical or rude, or simply ending the relationship even when things are going well. Often the cause behind this type of behavior is a deep-rooted fear of failure or nervousness around the idea of commitment. Rushing a relationship to its end before it has even had a chance to begin is rarely about the other person involved. Rather, it's usually the type of thing that someone does when they feel under confident about themselves or scared that they might hurt someone or be hurt by someone later on.

You can imagine what someone's relationship history might look like if self-sabotage is their Achilles heel. They might always leave relationships when things are going well, they might never being able to fully relax when in a relationship, they might not be able to trust other people fully, and they could be perpetually focused on the potential for future disaster. With things like that coursing through your mind, self-sabotage can seem like a fairly decent option. But how long can behavior like this go on without affecting your self-esteem? How many times can you hurt someone else by sabotaging your relationship with them before you end up hating yourself? Why are you letting fear get in the way of your happiness?

If some of this is ringing a bell for you, it might be time to start thinking about why. What underlying feelings or self-beliefs are causing you to keep people at arm's length? Are you afraid that you'll let them down in the future? Are you afraid that they won't accept you in your darker moments? Are you focusing too much on your flaws? Ask yourself: Can you accept love from someone else if you don't love yourself? Will you continue to question positive feelings other people have for you because you don't feel them for yourself? These are hard questions to face and my objective here is not to make you feel bad about yourself.

Rather, my aim is to encourage you to allow others to develop their own opinions of you. If we are ever going to have successful, long lasting relationships in our futures, we have to leave room for the possibility that someone else can love us, flaws and all. Loving us and accepting us is *their* decision, not ours. We have to be able to accept ourselves for who we are. We have to be able to let people in and trust them, or else we risk an increase in our social anxiety and even more experiences of isolation and defeat.

Self-sabotage can affect many things in our lives, not just our experiences in love. You might have a tendency to give up on yourself at work by turning up late or not turning up at all. You might be a student who is so scared of failing that you throw caution to the wind by not doing your work or staying up all night partying instead of studying. You might want to lose weight but every time you try to go on a diet, you end up eating even more and doing even less exercise because deep down, you're more afraid of failing than you are of being overweight.

Having a deep-rooted fear of failure is so much more complex than most of us know, because when we do self-sabotage, we rarely recognize it at the time. We tell ourselves lies and we make up excuses… *"My partner and I just want different things", "I don't even like this job", "Getting a degree is overrated anyway"*. It's important to be able to recognize when you're actually giving up because you're scared that you might not succeed in the end. Ending things before they even have a chance to begin is completely nonsensical. It is actively preventing yourself from going along with life's journeys, and it could very likely be a way to hold yourself back from potential happiness and success.

As our lives progress, the world will be hard enough on us. We will face challenges and defeats no matter who we are. We will experience heartbreak and disappointment. And in light of that, we have no excuse to make things even harder on ourselves. Things that are unpredictable will always be a little bit scary. Taking risks will always involve some nervousness. But what is life without a little adventure? What is life without risks?

5 - Trying to be someone you're not

Self-growth could be considered one of the greatest things about being human. We get to try different things, form opinions and reserve the right to change them later, learn new things, and take our lives in many different directions. But no matter how much you grow, you will always be you. There are some things that will always make you cringe, others that will always make you smile or frown. There are some political ideas that will never sit well with you, and others that you will believe in forever. Who we are at our core is not something to ignore or be ashamed of. You don't need to become an entirely different person in order to love yourself. We could all stand to be more compassionate and understanding with ourselves.

The problem arises when we try to be what we think other people want us to be. We try to impress people by saying what we think they want to hear. We hide our true thoughts and feelings because we're not sure what others will think of them. Now, I am not suggesting that you go around starting arguments with everyone you meet because you don't agree with something they've said. Nor should you ever feel like you have to oppose what other people are saying if it's likely to cause major problems in your relationship with them. What I'm saying is that we have to respect ourselves enough to be true to who we are. When we try to be something we're not, we're sending a message to ourselves and to the people around us that we don't like ourselves and we don't think we're good enough.

Not everyone you come across will want you to be perfect. In fact, most of us don't react well to people who act like they know everything. We respect the people we can relate to. Having flaws and faults are human qualities and being able to admit those things is a strength, not a weakness. When someone is talking about something you don't know a lot about, try admitting that you don't know much on the subject and ask them to tell you more. Doing this allows the person you're talking to, to feel good about themselves. It makes them feel useful. And this in turn, will make them want to talk to you more. It's not necessary to be an expert in everything in order to gain the respect of others. Being humble is far more likely gain you respect and admiration than you would obtain by being a know-it-all. So if you're inclined to alter your behavior and your personality when you're around other people, think less about impressing them and more about being relatable.

Remember that it's okay to have a difference of opinion. It's okay to have a different take on things. At the end of it all, there will always be some people who just don't like you; as harsh as that may sound. There will also be people that you don't like. This can be difficult for us to accept and it might be emotionally challenging when it happens, but it's true for all of us. Just keep in mind that it's not always necessary to win everyone over. Sometimes, you have to know when to call a spade and spade and spend your time with people who make you feel good about yourself rather than worrying about the few that don't.

As you come to the end of this section, you might want to continue focusing on some of the challenges I've already set for you so far. You might like to take them a step further or try some of the things you've found particularly difficult again. And there may be a few that you haven't gotten around to yet. Keep in mind that everyone will take a different amount of time to overcome these hurdles. There is no time limit when it comes to moving forward in life. We all will move at our own pace. In addition, most of the things I've encouraged you to do will need to be done a few times before you feel as though you've conquered them. But if you feel like you are ready for a new challenge, here's something you can implement into your life today:

Go to events you know you'll enjoy!
There is no point in forcing yourself to go places that you know are going to make you miserable. For instance, if you like things like movies and music, you might not be interested in going to a football game. If you like sports, you might be miserable sitting through a ballet. Remember that although it's great to try new things, if you're struggling with social anxiety, it might be best to focus on things you

really want to do so that you can begin your journey with positive experiences.

If there's a concert coming up that you know you'd enjoy, take the plunge and buy yourself a ticket! If there's a Scrabble night coming up and you happen to have a secret triple word score talent, sign up and give it a try! Have a look at upcoming events in your town and pick a few that sound intriguing to you. You can go alone or recruit a friend to go with you. While you're there, focus on *enjoyment*, and always give yourself credit when you conquer something new.

Case Study: Jeremy

Jeremy always thought of himself as "different". Growing up, he was nothing like the rest of his family. They called him an "oddball" and after a while that even became a pet name for him. "Where's the oddball this afternoon? What's the oddball going to do while we're out?" While his brothers and sisters went through the more common motions of growing up - little league, girl scouts, sleepovers, and sports - none of that was attractive to him. When his family went on outings, he preferred to stay at home alone, listening to music and drawing in his bedroom.

Things at school were even worse, because his nickname wasn't "oddball" there; it was "loser", "weirdo", "fag". Jeremy did his best to keep to himself throughout his school years. Socializing didn't feel like an option. He never went to a football game or a homecoming dance. He never raised his hand in class. He never had more than one friend at the time and those he did have, he couldn't fully trust. Most of them would end up back in the hateful crowd in no time, so it wasn't worth investing too much time and energy in them.

As he grew into adulthood, Jeremy's self esteem was painfully low. He continued to isolate himself and found it even harder to trust people. He'd gotten used to keeping people at arm's length and it was a hard habit to break. As a kid, isolating himself had been a way of keeping himself safe. But as an adult, things weren't quite that simple. Being isolated all the time made him deeply unhappy. And although he had always told himself that he was better off alone, the older he got, the lonelier he began to feel. Spending so many years basically living in hiding made it extremely difficult for him to socialize. Deep down, he was still afraid of ridicule. He was still afraid that no one would get him. He felt like he was stuck being an "oddball" for life. So he resisted integrating with others. Every time someone invited him out, he'd lie and say that he was busy. At work, he did the bare minimum even though he was capable of doing more. He had a bad attitude when working with other people. He'd become bitter and resentful. He felt on edge; angry and frustrated with life.

Continuing to believe that he was "different" than other people was Jeremy's way of self-sabotaging. By believing that other people would never understand or like him, he was keeping himself in the box his childhood peers had placed him in. Beneath the anger he felt for the masses, Jeremy was afraid. He had a fear of being made fun of, being bullied or rejected. But by refusing to integrate with others, he was only worsening his fear and resentment. Jeremy had to get the chip off his shoulder and face the world as an adult. He had to accept and celebrate the fact that all human beings are unique and that being "different" didn't have to be a bad thing. He had to believe that not everyone was out to get him and that there were more people like him in the world. He was his own saboteur and he needed to break free from the confines he had insisted on living in.

For Jeremy, just being able to realize these things for himself was a massive step in the right direction. Over a number of months, he would have to take some very small steps in order to reintegrate himself into the rest of the world. He had to accept that because he had been isolated for so long, the road ahead was going to be tough. But little by little, he learned how to treat himself kindly. With practice and time, he eventually stopped beating himself up and started loving himself.

Today, Jeremy is still making progress. He is more sociable than he ever was in the past but his anxiety hasn't entirely left him yet. He thinks of his journey as "putting himself back together". He is learning how to build himself up rather than constantly putting himself down. All in all, his view of the world has changed. He's realizes now that everyone is "different" and the reason he struggled with depression and anxiety his whole life, was because no one nurtured that part of him growing up. He knows now that being different isn't wrong, it's just being human. He is learning how to nurture the parts of himself that were neglected in his adolescence.

Practical Skills For Dealing With Social Anxiety Fast

So far, we've covered a lot of ground about how social anxiety affects you and where it comes from. You've been encouraged to take a few challenges along the way and you've learned a little bit about what types of behaviors might be making your anxiety hang around a little longer than you'd like. It's important to understand the theory behind some of our feelings and behaviors in order to get perspective, but it's also important to balance that theory with practical skills. Let's be honest, when you're in the middle of a social situation, there's not always enough time and space for you to sit and analyze your thoughts and feelings while they're happening. Most of that will have to wait until you have time later to reflect back on the situation at hand. In light of that, have a look over this next list to get a few practical skills under your belt. These are things that will help to make your social experiences as easy and successful as possible while you're in the moment.

Practical Skills For Successful Socializing

1 - Think realistically

Possibly the most important aspect of thinking realistically is having realistic expectations for yourself. If you're prone to being hard on yourself or beating yourself up for every mistake you make and every time you think you *should've* done something better, you might be setting your sights a little too high. If you can't think realistically and set tasks for yourself that you can actually achieve, you might risk lowering your self esteem and making it even harder to overcome your social anxiety. Having realistic expectations of yourself means being able to set yourself challenges that you're pretty sure you can overcome. For instance, if you are riddled with anxiety, you might want to start by going to a small get together with one or two friends rather than going to a large function where you're likely to feel intimidated by most of the guests. By doing this you are setting yourself up for a win, not a failure. When you set tasks for yourself that you know can face, you will be able to feel good about yourself and the experience afterwards, rather than throwing yourself into the deep end and beating yourself up later because you felt anxious the whole time.

So too, being dedicated to evaluating yourself and your progress through realistic eyes will always make you feel better than judging yourself too harshly. This means giving yourself credit for every small step forward, not ridiculing yourself for everything that doesn't quite go your way or kicking yourself for not feeling able to go further. Judging yourself fairly means focusing on you and your progress; not dwelling on how other people might feel or behave in the same situation. It means accepting your personal obstacles and giving yourself credit when you overcome them. Sometimes in life, we have to be our own cheerleaders. If you have a tendency to feel bad about yourself and give yourself a hard time, this is a skill that will serve you now and throughout the rest of your life.

It is important for us to be able to judge ourselves by our own criteria. For instance, let's say you have a sibling that seems to have everything. They have a high paying nine to five office job, a great house, and they get to take their family on all inclusive package vacations at least twice a year. But let's say that even though you're happy for your sibling, that's not really the life you want for yourself. Maybe you're a night owl and you prefer to work in the evening. Maybe you have a smaller home that has a lot of character and you love it. Maybe you're not really into going to the beach; you prefer going on more interesting vacations where you can soak up culture and look at great architecture.

Whatever your personal preferences are, if you judge your life by the criteria set by your sibling, you're bound to come up short. So you do beat yourself for not having what they have? Or might it be better to think about your own values and preferences and judge yourself by those? We have to be able to think about ourselves in the context us as individuals. What's easy for some people, will be hard for us. What other people don't have, we might have in abundance. Learning to accept this, and value yourself for who and what you are, is of paramount importance to how you view yourself in the world.

In addition, it's important to be able to realistically evaluate ourselves and the circumstances we're in. This way of thinking can have a positive impact on our self-beliefs as well as helping us gain perspective in difficult times. When anxiety is constantly chattering in your ear, it can be hard to accurately gauge the situation at hand. Just like that person who always gets panic attacks on the bus, anxiety has a way of tricking you into believing there's something to be afraid of when in fact, there is not. So we have to be able to quiet the voice of anxiety and amplify the voice of reason.

When you're in a social situation and your anxiety is telling you that there's danger present, summon up that voice of reason! Ask yourself a few questions to slow things down and get yourself thinking realistically. Ask yourself: Are people really staring at me or am I being paranoid? Am I the only person here that's feeling anxious or is it common to feel a twinge of anxiety in new surroundings? What is the worst thing that could happen? Is there anything here that's actually threatening? Is there any reason why I shouldn't try to lighten up and just enjoy this? Have you survived situations like this in the past? Again, the more you practice this type of self talk, faster and easier your anxiety will recede and you will be able to enjoy yourself.

2 - Be willing to laugh at yourself

Sometimes we all just need to lighten up and stop taking ourselves so seriously. Life doesn't have to just be about struggles and hardships. It doesn't have to be that negative. And when it comes to making that transition from the dark side to the light side, the power is in your hands. Yes, there are some people who just seem to be happy all the time and others who always seem to focus on the drearier parts of life. But every one of us has the power to either find a balance or switch sides completely.

Thinking about the heavier, more painful parts of life can easily become a habit. It can be a way for us to separate ourselves from others. And it can be a very addictive way of thinking. If you're used to feeling miserable, it will naturally be easier for you to summon up negative feelings than it will be to summon up positive ones. But life doesn't have to be like that. If you practice finding the positive things in life, you can just as easily turn that into a habit.

In life, we have to be able to laugh. We have to laugh at ourselves and the world in general. We get one life on this earth; there is absolutely no excuse to spend it wallowing. Anyone can lighten up. Try to recognize when you're taking life too seriously. If you're trapped in a negative thought cycle, try to break free from it and put it to rest. Focus on something lighter. Focus on enjoyment and warmth. Laugh about how ridiculous life can be sometimes. Look at yourself in the mirror and ask yourself if you're taking yourself too seriously. Now ask yourself if you'd like to have all that weight off your shoulders. Would you like feel lighter? Would you like to be able to just enjoy your life? Would you like to ditch your anxiety and be able to just go out and have fun? You can! You just have to let yourself.

Being light doesn't mean that bad things won't still happen. We will all go through struggles from time to time. Hardships will come and go. We will have conflicts, embarrassments, and losses. But what it really means to be light, is to give the good things in life the same amount of time and energy that we give to the negative stuff, if not more. Being able to laugh at yourself is an enjoyable way to get perspective. It's a way to shake off our failures, forgive ourselves for them, and move on. Laughter truly is great medicine. And not only does it help us heal, but it also helps us create healthy ties to other people.

3 - Be a good conversationalist

When it comes to social skills, being able to talk to people is crucial, but it's not always easy. In fact, being able to converse with comfort and confidence is often one of the hardest things for people with social anxiety to tackle. We can freeze up or become easily distracted by the changes in our body being caused by that almighty serge of excess adrenaline. In a busy room, we might feel like our senses are being over exerted. The noise, the smell of food and perfume, the constant motion of a social tide... all of it can have a dizzying effect on us. If you're trying to talk to someone with so much commotion around, it's easy to become distracted or disoriented. Although this can be extremely anxiety inducing, it might help to know that most people will feel similar in those situations, even if they don't suffer from social anxiety. Noisy rooms make it hard to think. On a practical level, when you're in a room like this, you might be best to keep conversation to small talk rather than struggling to be heard.

When it does come time to have more serious conversations, try not to focus too hard on what you're going to say next. Doing this might make you miss social cues or respond the wrong way to what other people are saying. Try to focus on *listening* and engaging with the person you're talking to. Remember that you don't have to have quick-fire responses to everything they say! You're allowed to speak slowly and to take your time if you're thinking of a reply. Doing this will make you appear and feel more comfortable and relaxed. It will also show the person you're talking to that you're invested in the conversation. If you reach a point where you're not sure what to say next, ask questions.

Ask them to further elaborate on a particular subject that you'd like to know more about. People respond well when you show a genuine interest in what they're saying. Asking more questions about something they've been telling you is akin to complimenting them. It's a way to say, "I like you. Keep talking!". If and when that moment passes, you can just revert to some basics. *How are things at work? How's the family? Ooh, where did you get that hat?* Whatever feels right in the moment.

Remember not to be antagonistic during a conversation. It's okay to disagree with people but try not to poke holes in everything they say. You don't have to verbalize every opposing opinion you hold. So too, note the tone of a conversation. If someone is talking about something serious, don't make jokes. If someone is joking, try to keep things light rather than bringing the tone down. Remember that you don't want to weigh people down with your problems or overwhelm them by talking *at* them. If you give someone a compliment, be sincere. Complimenting someone just for the sake of it won't always be received well, so make sure you mean what you say. And generally speaking, keep it clean. Keep your language and topic choices from straying anywhere south of PG-13. Most importantly, try to just enjoy yourself. Communicating with other people should be a pleasant experience, not something to dread or worry about.

4 - Fake it until you make it

As I mentioned briefly some time ago, often, just pretending that you're enjoying a social situation is enough to keep anxiety at bay. It might sound crazy but there is plenty of research to show that the more you smile, the happier you will feel. This theory is also true for negative emotions. If you frown or pretend that you're frustrated, you may actually start to feel that way. This is something that actors sometimes do to get into character. They make themselves feel a certain way so that their acting is more believable. So why not try this when it comes to social anxiety?

The next time you're in a social situation that would normally cause you to feel anxious - whether you're attending a party or simply going to the grocery store - put yourself in the mindset of someone who feels no anxiety in these situations. Pretend you're someone else. Let yourself smile and relax your jaw. Let your shoulders drop and ease any tension out of your neck. Keep your eyes up rather than looking at the ground. Let your arms and hands fall naturally at your sides rather than fidgeting or reaching for props. Walk slower than you normally would and let any feelings of urgency fall away. Doing this will make you appear less anxious but it might also make you feel more confident and at ease.

People like to be around happiness and light-heartedness. We like being around people that will have a positive effect on us. This is why we tend to gravitate toward people who seem confident and relaxed in themselves. We like to be near people who laugh and smile a lot. So if you can actually summon up those feelings by simply smiling more, why wouldn't you?

5 - Control your body language

Body language and facial expressions are powerful forces in social situations. When we're talking to someone in a one on one conversation, the way we sit, what we do with our hands, and what our face is doing will often express more than our words do. Like many other mammals, humans rely on posture, movement, and facial expressions to convey our feelings. If we're feeling shy or nervous, our eyes are usually lowered and our shoulders may curve forward as if to make us smaller. When we are proud, our spine is straight, our chests are open, and our chin is lifted. When we're angry, our jaw might clench, our gaze may become narrower, and the muscles in our neck and shoulders may tense up. But beyond these major bodily communications, there are quite a few minor ones. For instance, if we turn our bodies slightly away from the person we're speaking to, that usually means we're not entirely comfortable with them. If we fidget, we're probably nervous.

So how can we make sure our bodies are conveying the right messages? Imagine you are sitting across from someone at a table. If you're interested in that person or you like what they're saying, you might lean in towards them with your upper body or angle your entire body so that you're facing them. If you're not enjoying a conversation, you're likely to lean back and angle your body away from them. Further to that, if you want to appear less anxious, be careful not to close yourself off physically. This means not crossing your arms in front of your chest or holding your drink or any other props in front of your heart. When human beings feel threatened they will often subconsciously move in ways to protect their heart and chest, but doing this is a telltale sign that you're feeling intimidated. Maintaining an open and relaxed posture is a way of displaying confidence and inviting people to feel comfortable in your presence.

In order to keep your nerves from showing, try not to touch your face, hair, or neck too much. This is something human beings do to soothe themselves when they're feeling unsettled. Try to keep your hands still rather than constantly reaching for things or picking at your nails. Keep your eyes lifted rather than looking down when you're talking to someone. Don't stare or glare at them, just try to engage with them. Tilting your head slightly to the side and nodding along with them will also show that you are interested in what someone is saying. A small smile always makes people at ease. Just make sure that you don't keep smiling when someone tells you that their cat just died or they had a terrible day at work. Remember that even if you're using your body language to fake feeling comfortable, you might be able to convince yourself of that as well, so it's a win win!

6 - Know when you really don't want to be somewhere

As important as it is to push yourself out of your comfort zone and embrace social challenges, it's also important to be realistic. If we really don't want to be somewhere, we shouldn't have to force ourselves to go just because we're trying to overcome anxiety. Getting past your nerves doesn't mean you have to torture yourself! Let's face it, the more you go out and have a terrible time, the less you're going to want to do it again. We have to know when to trust our instincts. A lot of times, the reason we're feeling anxious in a social situation is because we just really don't want to be there. Suffering from social anxiety can make it hard for us to accurately gauge how we feel about a social situation. And if we feel the same panic and anxiety before *every* social event, identifying those feelings could be even harder.

The problem is that if you have a tendency to avoid socializing, it's easy to find excuses not to go somewhere. So how do we know if we genuinely don't want to go out? Start by being honest with yourself. What is it about the idea of going to this particular event that you're not into? Is it that you feel unsure about talking to people *(a.k.a. social anxiety)* or that you genuinely don't like the people that are going to be there *(a.k.a. you don't want to be there)?* Are you worried about how you look or what people will think of you *(a.k.a. social anxiety)* or do you hate the band that's playing *(a.k.a. you don't want to be there)?*

Being able to think a bit deeper about your feelings before heading out for the night can be a helpful skill to have on your side. If you're able to realistically judge the feelings beneath your intensions, you'll be more able to decide whether your anxiety is holding you back or this particular event just isn't for you. Sometimes you will experience a combination of anxiety and really not wanting to go out, such as if you're likely to run into an ex, and it's important to go easy on yourself in situations like these. You might not be ready to face that person yet and that is absolutely fine. Events that pose extra challenges like that will probably take a little bit of extra work. Learn to accept that taking baby steps is a good thing.

Approaching social anxiety like this will encourage you to conquer smaller things first and build up to bigger things later. This mean that you'll be able to feel good about your accomplishments and gain confidence as you go along, rather than forcing yourself to do things that are likely to set you back. If you do have a setback, don't be too hard on yourself. These journeys are different for everyone and there's no need to beat yourself up if yours takes a little longer than you expected. Go easy on yourself and remember to treat yourself like a friend.

7 - Focus on having fun

As I have said time and time again, socializing should be fun. When we're coping with social anxiety, it can be easy to miss opportunities for genuine enjoyment, so we have to remember to leave room for the possibility that we might actually be able to have some fun while we're out. There is a reason people have parties and celebrations. There is a reason we like going to concerts and sports matches. Human beings are made to share their lives with others. We are at our most productive when we work in groups. We are meant be there for each other in times of celebration and in times of mourning. Try not to think of other people as enemies. Try not to think of yourself as "different" or unworthy. We all have to let go and blow off steam sometimes. We all need things in our lives that are strictly for the purpose of having fun. Playing is a one of our basic fundamental needs, and this is not supposed to stop when we reach adulthood. Try to remember that life can be fun - that it *has* to be fun sometimes.

So whenever you notice yourself taking things a little too seriously, try to gain some perspective. Ask yourself: Is this social outing really important enough to have you wracked with nerves? Are you about to accept an academy award or are you just hanging out with friends? Are you running for president or just going shopping? Should every social experience be allowed to rob you of all positive emotions?

Does everything have to be so serious all the time? Having fun is a great way to lower you stress levels, help you maintain a positive outlook on life, ensure happier and more productive relationships, and lengthen your life span. Plus, the more you engage in enjoyable socializing, the better you'll feel about yourself and the world around you.

8 - Be in the moment

I often talk about the importance of letting yourself just be present. This means letting go of things that live in the past and the future. Worrying about what might happen tomorrow or next year is rarely productive. And holding onto embarrassment, shame and regret keeps us rooted in the past. We have to be able to exist in the here and now and let ourselves have each moment while we're actually living it. This means not letting anxiety steal the moment away from you. It means keeping perspective on your anxiety and knowing when it's valid versus when it's not.

Remember that anxiety actually does serve a purpose. It helps alert us to potential danger. It has the power to ramp up our adrenaline which is great when we need a little extra strength to conquer something like working out in the gym or problem solving. But we have to be able to recognize when anxiety is serving us versus when it's preventing us from living our lives. Practicing being in the moment can help take the sting out of anxiety. It bears repeating that every time you feel yourself worrying about what *might happen*, you are missing out on what *is happening*.

Your anxiety shouldn't be allowed to have that power over you. It shouldn't be allowed to dictate when you can enjoy yourself and when you can't. So anytime you feel your anxiety leading you astray, try to pull your mind back to the present. Try to slow things down and get your focus back. Don't let yourself dwell on what has already passed or what is yet to come. Give yourself the freedom to simply be in the moment you're in.

Making and Maintaining Relationships

I have often said that sharing the earth with other human beings can simultaneously be our greatest comfort and our greatest challenge in life. The way we relate to people can have a dramatic impact on how we feel about ourselves. It can be the primary cause of social anxiety as well as causing difficulties with mood, ineffective communication, and poor mental health. When we are treated badly, we may struggle with low self-esteem or become withdrawn. But when our time with others is a positive force in our lives, it can help us to feel like we aren't alone. If we feel supported and appreciated by others, we will naturally feel better about ourselves and the world around us. We are at our best when we feel valued and respected.

Without sufficient positive human contact, we are likely to feel depressed and isolated. We may not feel as though our existence important. We mightn't feel like we truly belong anywhere. We need to be able to help others and be helped by others. We need to love and be loved. We need to belong to - and be able to contribute to - something bigger than ourselves. These are all facets of our most basic primal needs.

But making and maintaining relationships is far from basic. In fact, maintaining relationships can take a lot of effort at times. Up until now, I have encouraged you to celebrate the fact that we are all unique, but it's important to note that this particular attribute of being human can make relating to other people pretty complicated at times. Beyond our fundamental needs, human beings vary greatly. Unfortunately, our values don't just spring from our animal instincts.

Rather, we absorb and develop wildly varying opinions, knowledge, ideas, and beliefs throughout our lives. Our value systems are informed by our own experiences and often, the things we believe in can have the power to separate us from others in dramatic ways. The intensity with which we can reason and moralize is one of the most defining differences between us and the rest of the animal kingdom. For humans, it's not always the "runt" of the litter that gets rejected. Unfortunately, things for us are far more complex than that.

It is incredible just how much our relationships shape who we are; from our primary caregivers in childhood to the people we meet through school and work, to our extended family, and not least, our friends and lovers. Keeping relationships on good terms can take a lot of work. Even when two people know each other their entire lives, they are likely to have many different experiences and emotional triggers. To illustrate this best, let's think about the relationship between two siblings. Imagine two children living in the same house from the day they are born until they reach adulthood. Does the fact that they share their home life mean that they will grow up to have the same values, strengths, and weaknesses? Of course not.

They may develop some similarities to each other but even if they go to the same school with the same teachers and they share the same friends, they will still grow up to be different individuals. The relationship between them will still go through ups and downs. A shared childhood will not shield them from that aspect of relating to one another. Between them, they may experience conflict, betrayal, and pain as well as triumph, love, and unity. But if they don't have the skills they need to keep their relationship strong and healthy, the negatives may begin to outweigh the positives. Without having the desire to stay connected to each other and understanding how to maintain an equally beneficial relationship, they may end up going separate ways in adulthood.

The importance of healthy relationships in our lives is not something to be underestimated. Even when we prefer to be alone, we all need support and understanding at times. We all need to feel *liked*. We are not born to be lone wolves. And if our experiences with relationships are mostly negative, the likelihood of us developing social anxiety will increase. If we're not comfortable meeting new people, we won't feel comfortable in social spheres. If we can't effectively maintain friendships, familial ties, and intimate relationships, socializing will naturally be more difficult. Furthermore, if we have negative experiences in relationships, our self-esteem might suffer, we may develop poor self-beliefs, and we might become withdrawn, resentful, or bitter. All of these things have the power to worsen social anxiety.

Having a poor relationship history does not have to be a life sentence. Negative experiences do not always repeat themselves. If you want to be able to maintain relationships better in your future, you can. There's nothing worse than going to an event where you might run into someone you'd rather not see. Very few things can ramp up anxiety like running into someone with whom you've had a bad experience. But wouldn't you love the ability to see that person and not be phased by their presence? Wouldn't it be so freeing to not have to worry about who's going to be at a party before deciding if you're going to go to it or not? Would you like to be able to socialize with people despite the possibility that things between you may have been strained in the past? Most importantly, would you like to have healthy relationships in your future? What would it look like to have strong ties to your friends and family members? What would an intimate relationship be like without jealousy, suspicion, and constant conflict?

Throughout this book, I have encouraged you to try to *be curious* about other people's thoughts and feelings, and I cannot stress just how much learning to do this can positively impact on your relationships. Being curious means thinking about what's going on in someone else's head rather than being overly focused on how their actions reflect on you. This is a skill that takes a long time to perfect but when it comes to maintaining relationships and being solid in who you are, it may be one of the most useful things you'll ever learn.

For many people, especially those who have struggled with depression, low self-esteem, and/or personality disorders, it can feel like everyone is out to get you. It can feel like no one understands what things are really like for you and that everything in the world is happening *to you*. Other people can make you feel agitated or frustrated. And when someone says something that doesn't quite fit with your experience, it can feel like they are disbelieving, unsupportive, or patronizing. Often, when other people try to help you, it can seem more like they're being condescending and judgmental.

Feeling emotionally activated by people or opinions that differ from your own and/or feeling as though no one fully understands what things are like for you, can be described as having a *narcissistic defense*. Unlike classic narcissism where a person is entirely focused on themselves at all times, having a narcissistic defense is more about being particularly sensitive when it comes to receiving criticism and/or accepting help. For instance, imagine that someone else is good at something that you're not great at. They might try to help you with it but your deep-rooted insecurity might cause you to react with a narcissistic defense. You may become angry, spiteful, or overly negative. You might lash out or think badly of them because in a way, it's easier to place your focus on them than it is to admit your own weakness.

But that's only the tip of the iceberg. Someone with a narcissistic defense might also become emotionally activated when other people accomplish things that they haven't, or when other people don't react the way want them to at any given moment. Hearing the words, "everything isn't about you" might cause extreme outrage. None of us want to be thought of a self-centered. However, in the context of narcissistic defense, knowing that everything isn't about you can be a very positive thing to hold onto. Because rather than always feeling that the things other people say and do are a reflection or comment on *you* and *your* decisions, being able to recognize when things aren't about you can mean feeling less attacked, less judged, and less angry in general. It can make accepting and respecting others a lot easier, hence making your experiences with them more positive and enjoyable. Learning to drop one's narcissistic defense and adopt a posture of being curious, means that you are able to accept that the way other people behave is about *them*, not about you. Learning how to be genuinely happy for other people is a virtue. It means being able to let go of our insecurities, accept ourselves as we are in the here and now, and be gracious towards others. In means understanding that other people's accomplishments stand alone; they do not reflect on what you have or haven't accomplished.

Often when someone thinks, says, or does something a different way than we do, it can make us get worked up. We might feel challenged, judged, or even hurt. But we need to be strong enough in who we are to be able to accept that other people will inevitably be different. We need to be able to accept help and criticism without feeling as though we've failed. We need to be able to follow our own path with confidence and self-assuredness. We must accept that some people will struggle in life while others may not. That is simply the nature of human existence. It's chaotic and senseless at times. We have to choose whether that fact will lead us on a path of spite and cynicism or a path of grace and quiet understanding.

Maintaining relationships often means accepting things about other people that you might not like. We have to be able to value other people's feelings and leave room for the possibility that they might differ from our own. The next time you experience a conflict with someone, try to be curious about what is happening in their mind. Do they feel attacked? Are they perhaps a little bit insecure and exhibiting a narcissistic defense themselves? Has something triggered them or made them act defensively? Are they having a bad day? Might they have a headache? Are they feeling low? Are they simply set in their ways? If someone reacts differently to something than you would've, does that make their feelings any less valid? Most importantly, is it okay to agree to disagree and move on without feeling hurt or upset?

Think back to the example at the beginning of this book when Rebecca was "blanked" by an acquaintance on the street. With her narcissistic defense wielded like an emotional battle shield, it would've been easy for Rebecca to feel like she had been blanked on purpose. No matter what had actually caused that person to walk by her, it was happening *to her*. It had to have been *about her*. It would've been all too easy for her to get swept up in a flurry self focus and believe that there was a conflict where there mightn't have been one at all. In our minds, any tiny occurrence can become monumental. But by dropping the narcissistic defense and adopting a curious stance, Rebecca was able to leave room for the possibility that the person who blanked her may have had other things going on that had nothing to do with her. They might've been late for a meeting, or they might've been trying to remember everything they had to get at the grocery store. You get the gist.

Being able to relate to people and to remain secure in who we are, is at the crux of successful socialization. What other people do is about them. What you do is about you. And the more good will you have toward others, the more you will be able to genuinely celebrate their personal triumphs without feeling defensive or insecure. Being able to rise above the little things will make your relationships more balanced and your self-confidence more solid.

Relationships & Anxiety

Anxiety is an all encompassing feeling. It can skew your view of reality. It can make you feel like you're the only person on the planet. It can make your thoughts race so fast that what you're experiencing is the only thing on your mind. It might seem like everyone else fades into the background. At a party, you might not be able to get out of your own head long enough to realize that everyone else there is having thoughts and feelings of their own. Many of them may also be struggling with anxiety, conflict, or fear of running into someone they don't want to see.

Although it may be a hard lesson to take on board, being secure enough in yourself to accept that everything other people say and do is not about you, can make relating to them a lot easier. Being able to slow your thinking down and be curious about how other people are feeling is a huge part of being able to keep your relationships healthy and getting over your social anxiety. If you go out to a party and your ex happens to be there, leave room for the possibility that they might feel just as nervous and uncomfortable as you do. If they've moved on and you haven't yet, that doesn't mean that you have failed in any way. Their life is not a reflection on yours. If your sister gets snappy with you, it might not be because of something you did or didn't do; she might've just had a bad night's sleep or she might be stressed out at work. Everything doesn't have to be so intense all the time.

It's important to know how to bend a little. Being too ridged with your opinions or your beliefs can lead to conflict in relationships and difficulties where socializing is concerned. Disagreements do happen and they will continue to happen as long as we live. But if we're not careful, our disagreements can lead to more serious trouble. Whether you're striking up a new friendship with someone you've just met or you're in a long-term intimate relationship, being able to compromise is a virtue. Compromising doesn't mean letting go of your beliefs and it doesn't mean losing a fight.

It's simply a lot easier to ensure successful, enjoyable social encounters when we leave room for the possibility that others will not agree with everything we say and do. For longer, mutually beneficial relationships we have to actively accept and respect the differences between us and the people we spend time with. We have to embrace their uniqueness and individuality to the same degree that we would like them to do for us.

As I'm sure you know, not all people have a hard time compromising. Some of us are actually a little bit too compromising. Within the minefield of relationships, being able to strike a balance is key. If you think of yourself as someone who people often take advantage of, your tendency to compromise could be hurting you. It doesn't feel good to be a doormat for your friends and family. It doesn't feel good to be mistreated or bossed around. And being treated like inferiors certainly does not boost our confidence. If this is how things are for you, it's no wonder socializing causes you so much grief! Many people who struggle with feelings of low self worth, enter relationships with people that are particularly dominant.

They may have family members who have always treated them poorly or they might work in an office full of people who are endlessly condescending. They might feel used and abused by their friends or they may end up in emotionally manipulative relationships with their lovers. Depending on your background and the nature of your early relationships, you may be affected by cycles of abuse. The problem is that if you're used to being on the bottom of the totem pole, it can be pretty hard to climb to the top.

Learning to value yourself, your needs, and your personal beliefs is vital if you ever want to establish healthy, respectful relationships. If you have struggled with being assertive where these things are concerned, it might be time to give it another try. We should all be allowed to express our feelings without fear of ridicule or rejection. We should be able to think and feel differently than the people in our life without being scared of losing them or feeling as though they are somehow above us. One-sided relationships can be seriously damaging to your sense of self and to your mental wellbeing.

We all deserve to be heard. But if we don't value ourselves, no one else will either. Therefore, we need to be able to set boundaries that will keep us safe and happy in our relationships. And we have to be able to tell people when they do things that hurt us. We have to be able to say no to people who take advantage of us. If you are the type of person who is always there for your friends but they are rarely there for you, it might be time to set some boundaries. Allowing yourself to be drained or hurt by your friends because you're afraid to upset them, will not make you feel great about yourself or your friendships in the long run. Learning to care for yourself means knowing your personal limits and protecting yourself from harmful relationships. It means being able to assert your feelings and having them be respected by the people in your life. Creating healthy boundaries means taking care of number one, first.

This might mean that you don't talk about certain subjects with people who are likely to be insensitive or make you feel bad about yourself. It might mean saying no to helping a friend if you have other plans. Or it might mean being able to prioritize your own needs and not being available for other people all day every day. Although some people in your life might take some time to come around to the changes you make, a true friend will respect you enough to encourage you, or at least accept that you need to focus on you sometimes. It might be hard to see the connection between relationships and social anxiety but it's actually quite simple. Being in healthy relationships creates healthy self-esteem, which in turn makes socializing infinitely easier and more enjoyable.

Getting out of bad relationship patterns is key to having a healthy social life. We all have to deal with people that are difficult from time to time and knowing how to navigate situations like that is a great skill to add to your repertoire. So what do you do with people who are bossy, overly negative, hurtful, or passive aggressive? It may help to be curious about what's going on with them so that you can try to gain some perspective. But you also need to know how to protect yourself from being affected by their negativity. It can be a tricky balance to strike, but it is possible to be a good friend without sacrificing yourself in the process.

Recognize when you need to take some time to focus on yourself. You deserve to do things that are important to you. If you're feeling low and one of your friends is in need, it's okay to tell your friend that you care about them but that you need to look after yourself for a while. If they can't handle that or they give you a hard time about it, that's their problem. Sometimes you're better off saving your energy for yourself.

Think of people as drains and radiators. There are some people who drain you of all your energy and others who provide you with warmth and comfort. Generally speaking, you'll be better off by spending the majority of your time with radiators. If there are some drains in your life, protect yourself by limiting how often you see them or not talking about things that might trigger a conflict with them. Remember that if someone is overly critical of you, it's probably got more to do with them than it does with you. Be strong enough in yourself to withstand their criticism and if you've had enough, remember that you're allowed to be assertive about that.

You don't have to engage them in an argument, just politely ask to change the subject. It's okay to say that you don't think this conversation is going anywhere productive. If they still won't stop talking about it, tell them again. Agree to disagree and move on. In the future, avoid that topic with that person. This is what we mean when we think about setting boundaries. Creating and maintaining boundaries means being able to recognize when relationships are having a negative effect on you and making some subtle alterations in order to protect yourself from being drained.

If you are involved in any relationships that you think might not be working out, it's probably worth reevaluating them. Staying in relationships that are hurtful, overly negative, abusive, or manipulative can be extremely damaging to your mood and your self-esteem. The longer you remain in relationships like this, the more likely you are to develop similar relationships in the future. Ending relationships is never easy, but it's rarely worth staying in a relationship just because you're afraid of what's on the other side. Unhealthy relationships can very possibly be the cause of your social anxiety.

Think of it this way, if you spend enough time with someone who makes you feel bad about yourself, it's only natural that you will find socializing daunting. If you spend enough time with someone who doesn't value you, you're going to be less likely to value yourself. Relationships have a profound impact on who we are and how we view ourselves in the world, and sometimes, they just don't work out. Endings take bravery and courage. Yes, they can be horrible, but they are temporary. We all deserve more out of life than we can achieve by remaining in relationships that are causing us pain. This is *your* life and you deserve to value it.

Remember that when you're meeting new people and starting new relationships, try to steer yourself towards "radiators". So too, if there are people in your life who are warm and caring, who make you feel good about yourself, spend more time with them! It's wonderful to be able to feel light around other people. It's nice to be able to take joy from the simple things in life, especially when you share them with likeminded individuals. And if you want to overcome your social anxiety, surrounding yourself with the right kind of people can help in leaps and bounds.

For the purpose of being proactive in your self-progression, take some time over the next week or so to evaluate your relationships. Think about your friends, family members, and lovers. Think about if they are good for you or bad for you and after you've done that, try to identify what it is about these relationships that make you feel the way you do. Think of any boundaries you might need to set in order to turn your negative relationships into positive ones. Are there certain topics you should avoid with someone? Is there someone you need to see a little less often? Do you need to try saying no to someone who takes advantage of you? Is there someone who's overly critical of you that you might need to talk to about that? What qualities do you value in another person? Are there people in your life that you'd like to spend more time with? Is it possible that you might benefit from meeting some new people?

It's important to remember that the world is full of people you haven't met yet and even though the majority of us rarely make new friends in our mid to late adulthoods, it is still possible to do so. As we focus on self-progression, certain things about us will change and it is possible that we might outgrow some of our friends. Feeling as though you have surpassed someone in one way or another can feel a bit strange; it might even make you feel a little bit guilty. But self-progression isn't easy and when you've put so much time and dedication into feeling better about yourself, you deserve better things in life. Sometimes that will mean taking a step back from people in your life. Other times it will mean stepping forward and making ties with new people.

Coping With Rejection

Rejection can be one of the hardest things to contend with in life. The feelings involved with rejection can include anger, defeat, grief, worthlessness, embarrassment, and number of other difficult emotions. Rejection is a part of all of our lives and it can range from experiences as simple as being criticized for what you're wearing to being turned away by someone you love. If your childhood and/or teenage years involved being rejected by a parent or other primary caregiver, you may have grown up to be particularly sensitive when it comes to rejection. So too, if you have undergone a rejection in adulthood which you found particularly difficult to cope with, such as a divorce or the ending of a long-term friendship, you may also be predisposed to nervousness when it comes to letting yourself be loved and accepted by others. You may be wary of people who show an interest in you.

You might be more guarded than other people or you could end up diving head first into relationships and getting hurt later. If you have struggled with rejection in the past, it's almost inevitable that it will continue to be a source of contention in your life. It's important to know that there is nothing right or wrong when it comes to your feelings. For those of us who are a little more sensitive when it comes to receiving negative feedback, coping with rejection is bound to be upsetting and hard to recover from. Beating yourself up about that will not help. You are not broken or weak.

If you had a difficult or abusive childhood, or if you've struggled with depression or anxiety throughout your life, you may have grown up to be a sensitive individual. And if that is the case, it is vital for you to learn to maintain perspective when other people don't appreciate you and your accomplishments. Having past experiences with rejection can make you more prone to seek approval from others. If you had a neglectful parent for instance, your need for approval might be more exaggerated than others. If you were bullied or mocked at any time in your life, you might be particularly sensitive to criticism.

For people with these or similar backgrounds, simply approving of yourself mightn't feel like it's enough to keep your head held high. You might be prone to viewing yourself in a negative light. We all need to be approved of and appreciated but if we can't offer ourselves that same approval and appreciation, we will continue to let other people's judgements rule how we feel about ourselves. This is a very fragile state to exist in. And if you do struggle to cope with rejection, socializing can be excruciatingly difficult. The fear of being judged can be all consuming.

If you have a deep-rooted need for approval, it's more than likely that you'll be overly critical of yourself. You might not be able to exist in a social setting without constantly thinking about what other people think of you. What you look like, what you're wearing, what's going on in your life, how you spend your time, who you like, who you love… all of these things about *you* might feel like they're being placed in the hands of *others* to be approved of or rejected. But when you are able to approve of yourself, these things can remain in your hands. When you're able to judge yourself realistically and hold your head high, other people's opinions won't carry so much weight.

Rejection happens in almost every sphere of life. Our ideas at work may be rejected, our loved ones mightn't be receptive or respectful of us, our friends may be overly judgmental of the choices we make, and we might be forced to endure the breaking up of relationships that we thought would last forever. If you're single and you get into Internet dating, you might feel like you're going through rejection in rapid succession. You're flying high one day and hitting rock bottom the next. Meeting new people can be uncomfortable and nerve wracking. Plus, the politics of texting and emailing can be torturous. We subject ourselves to rejection all day long when posting tales of our to's and fro's online. Waiting for someone to hit that "like" button when you've posted something funny might be your best attempt at boosting your self-esteem in any given moment. *They liked my post, that must mean they like me. No one liked my post, that means I'm not as funny or smart as I thought I was.*

Our need for instant gratification can have the power to make us love or hate ourselves in mere moments. For people who are sensitive or who happen to be in a period of low mood, enduring judgement like this can lead you through a labyrinth of mixed emotions and flimsy self-beliefs. Without having a solid sense of self and strong feelings of self-confidence, experiences of rejection can have terrible effects on us.

So what can we do when rejection comes knocking at our door? As usual, you can start by being curious about what's happening for the other person. Might their rejection of you is actually a show of their own insecurities? Are they trying to get a rise out of you? Have they even considered that their actions might be affecting you negatively? Try slowing your thoughts down and thinking realistically. Even if someone is being critical of you, does that mean that your view of yourself has to change? Does it mean that you should feel embarrassed?

Do you have to avoid that person or that subject from now on? Is agonizing over it going to help or might it be better to take the hit, get back up, and move on? Remember that the more perspective you can get and the more steady you feel in yourself, the less likely you will be to get caught in the net of rejection and succumb to negativity and self doubt.

Ultimately, being able to cope with rejection means being strong in who you are. It means being able to approve of yourself, feeling confident about the things you do, and being able to withstand criticism. If you have difficulties coping with rejection, it is likely for that to have taken root at the center of your social anxiety. You will never be fully comfortable in social settings if you're scared of rejection and criticism. At the end of the day, you have to try to grow a thicker skin. Try not to let other people's opinions negate your own. When someone makes a passing comment that you find hurtful, try not to get swept away in its wake.

Ask yourself: Did they mean to hurt you? How do *you* feel about the thing they criticized you for? Is it okay for people to have a different take on things than you do? Does another person's negative outlook have to change the way you feel about yourself or can approving of yourself be enough? If you like something that other people don't like, is that a flaw or is it just a symptom of individuality?

We all need to feel liked and approved of but not everyone is going to get on board with everything we say and do. Being able to rise above moments of disapproval means that you'll be able to live your life they way you want to. It means that you can feel confident in your choices regardless of what other people think. The best approval is that which we can give ourselves.

It's important to be able to recognize when someone is trying to be helpful with their criticism. If someone isn't totally on board with something you're doing, try to leave room for the possibility that they are not rejecting you as such; they might just want to share their take on it. You don't have to take other people's advice if you don't want to. You can just let it wash over you.

But also remember that taking someone's advice doesn't mean that you've failed. It can be hard not to get defensive but there is great strength in being able to accept people's advice graciously. Try to keep yourself open to other people's ideas without letting them bog you down. When it comes to other people's take on your life, just take the good stuff and leave the bad. Trust yourself enough to use what's useful and toss the other things to the side.

There will also be times when someone will be overly critical of you because their own insecurities are getting the better of them. If someone feels threatened by you, intimidated or jealous, they might pick on you just for the sake of it. And although this can be ugly and hurtful at times, being able to hold onto that perspective means that the things they say don't have to hit your self-esteem. Remember that every failure you endure, every rejection you suffer, does not have to alter the way you feel about yourself. You are a human being and you will make mistakes. None of us are perfect. None of us do the right thing all the time. Sometimes we do things that are embarrassing. Sometimes we aren't our best selves. Sometimes people just don't get us.

This is a risk we take when we enter the social sphere. But we have to be able to judge ourselves realistically. We have to be able to love and respect ourselves no matter what other people think of us. When someone is criticizing your work, ask yourself if you feel like you've done it to the best of your ability. When someone judges your hair or clothes, ask yourself if you were happy with them before you left the house. That's what matters! Navigating our social lives takes resilience. And resilience takes practice and patience. Rather than letting other people tear you down, focus on building yourself up. Practice slowing your thinking down, gaining perspective, and maintaining your positive feelings.

Finally, if there are people in your life who are consistently judgmental or rude, it might be time to do something about it. If it's a family member or a close friend whom you'd like to keep in your life, you'll need to think about being assertive with your feelings. Confrontation and conflict are never easy but if someone's thoughts or actions are getting you down, you'll be better off telling them about it than you would be if you allowed it continue. Not all conflict has to be dramatic. You can have a formal sit down with them if you want to, but you could also just simply mention your feelings in a passing comment.

If you're conversing with that person and they throw a rude comment your way, just say, *"Can you please stop criticizing me? I really don't like when you do that"*. That just might be enough to open a dialogue about it and nip it in the bud. If you don't think that will work in your situation, remember that you can always pare back what things you share with that person. Some people will always be flippant and careless with your feelings. And it's important to remember that not everyone is willing to change. Being able to accept that about a person can really change how you feel about your relationship with them.

At the end of the day, if you know that someone will always be rude to you about certain things, try to steer clear of those subjects with them. Don't let their tendency to disapprove of you intercept or negate the approval you feel for yourself.

Case Study: Maggie

Maggie grew up as a victim of child neglect. Her parents divorced when she was a baby and at that time, it was decided that she would reside with her mother and step father. The divorce was angry and hateful and Maggie was forced to listen to her parents speak badly of one another for years. But in addition to that somewhat average experience of being a child of divorce, Maggie's mother wasn't naturally maternal. She was self centered and did not have the capacity to raise Maggie the way a mother should. She lacked warmth and compassion; and as the years went by she had very little to do with her daughter at all. From the age of eight, Maggie was forced to do her own laundry. She was expected to cook her own meals by the age of twelve. Coming from a middle class household where she was provided with ample food, shelter, and clothing meant that none of Maggie's teachers or friends guessed what things were like at home. She didn't show the classic signs of abuse so her struggles went unnoticed.

As many children of neglect do, Maggie did everything in power to try to win her mother's approval. She desperately wanted to be loved by her. She wanted to feel special and cared for. But her mother's approval never came. Maggie's accomplishments were not celebrated, her efforts never rewarded. She felt like she was invisible. And as is almost always the case, the subconscious "relationship blueprint" that Maggie developed as a result of her relationship with her mother later dictated how she would relate to others.

As she grew into a young adult, Maggie never had a friendship that lasted longer than a few months. Her love life was tumultuous and often left her in terrible throes of heartbreak and depression. The relationship she'd had with her mother had become a pattern. She fell in love with people who rarely reciprocated her feelings; people that she had to chase for their love. When someone did love and appreciate her, she found it hard to trust them and almost never allowed them to get close to her. The deep need for approval she'd once felt with her mother, repeated itself in most of her relationships. She needed other people to validate her existence. She simply could not approve of herself. She had virtually no sense of self as an independent woman; no great feelings of confidence or pride. And what was worse was that she'd grown up surrounding herself with people just like her mother. People who would never love her the way she needed to be loved. People who judged her harshly and who abandoned her once she'd developed an attachment to them.

As a result of growing up in an unstructured and insecure environment, Maggie grew up to be emotionally fragile and unsure of herself. She was uncomfortable in group settings and awkward around people in general. She was needy by nature. When she was ready to make a change in her life, she had a lot to overcome. But the hardest thing would be conquering her need for approval and becoming resilient in the face of criticism and rejection. She needed to learn how to approve of herself and let that be enough. She needed to be able to accept criticism without devastation.

She started by recognizing her relationship pattern. It hadn't occurred to her that the reason she couldn't maintain relationships was because of how she'd been treated by her mother. Once she was able to see that, things got a lot clearer. She had to stop thinking of all people as being better than her. She had to understand that she was not incapable of having long lasting relationships. She just needed to retrain her instincts where people were concerned and get some practice. She needed to be able to accept love and affection rather than chasing people who would never give her the love she needed.

It took a few years for Maggie to fully recover from her neglectful childhood but she did manage to come through the process as a happy, healthy, well-rounded woman. She spent the majority of those years reflecting on every experience she had with other people and seeking to understand why they made her feel the way they did. She constantly asked herself if the way she was feeling in the present had something to do with her past. She spent a lot of her time learning how to be good to herself. That meant treating herself kindly, doing things for her own enjoyment, and most of all, learning to approve of herself.

These days Maggie has a strong support network. She has ended most of her co-dependent relationships and replaced them with relationships built on solid ground. She has learned how to set boundaries to keep herself emotionally safe. Her transformation has been truly unbelievable. She got her life back! And now that she no longer seeks the approval of others, Maggie loves socializing. Spending time with people no longer feels desperate, awkward, or needy. She doesn't worry so much about what other people think of her. She no longer views herself as less worthy than other people. She knows now what she has to offer the world.

The Fear Of Rejection Can Be Defeated

Thinking about how rejection features in our lives can be a powerful exercise. Many times, beneath our insecurities, frustration, anxiety, and resentment there lies a deep-rooted fear of not being good enough. A fear of failure can haunt us and determine how we live our lives. But as you learned in the last section, we need to resist thinking about ourselves and our accomplishments *emotionally*, and instead, we need to be able to make these assessments *realistically*. We need to be able to evaluate ourselves based on our own criteria. Otherwise, we risk continued ill feelings where other people are concerned and heightened social anxiety.

If you find that other people's actions or choices make you feel frustrated, try to think about why that is. Do they do things differently than you would? If so, why does that bother you so much? Deep down, do their actions make you feel insecure about your own? When people speak positively about their lives, do you often view it as bragging? If so, what feelings are beneath that? Is there an insecurity beneath your frustration? Do other people's accomplishments remind you of the things you haven't yet accomplished? Do their choices make you question your own?

It can be hard to admit - or even identify - when our surface feelings are actually a mask for something deeper. As we go through life, we will make mistakes and we will have struggles. But some things can be really hard for us to let go of. For instance, if you were once financially successful but ended up losing it all, you might find it hard to celebrate someone else's financial success because of the insecurity or grief you still hold around that issue. Or, if you were once happily married and your partner cheated on you, you might become cynical or flippant when a friend tells you that they're getting married. Losses and failures from your past can cause massive amounts of devastation and shame, but they happen to us all. And when they do, it's not uncommon to feel angry with the world. It's natural to feel a bit triggered when someone else is on top and you're buried beneath shame and disappointment.

However, we do not have to be defined by our failures! No matter what we've suffered, we all have the capacity to bounce back. We can learn and grow from our mistakes. We can forgive ourselves and start over. There is no need to carry that old negativity around with you everywhere you go. What's gone is gone. We have to be able to let go and focus on life in the here and now. We have to be able to accept that our friends' lives are not a reflection of our own. We have our own values, standards, and criteria from which we can create the lives we want for ourselves. What other people do is their business.

The ability to stop comparing yourself to other people can be of massive benefit when it comes to getting over social anxiety. When you're in a social situation and your anxiety is peaking, you won't be thinking of things like rejection and relationships. You're more likely to feel overwhelmed, fearful, and on edge. This is when you need to lean on the practical skills you now possess. But in those times when things are quiet and calm, reflecting on your deeper thoughts and concerns means that you will be able to get to the root of the problem. If anxiety was a weed in your garden, would it be better to take it down with a lawnmower and let it grow back in a week's time, or would you rather uproot it entirely so you know it'll be gone for good? This is what I mean to achieve when I encourage you to dig a bit deeper. Any pamphlet or webpage can list a few tips and tricks to help you calm down when you're panicking, but there will come a time when you'll be ready to free yourself completely. Because letting anxiety own you, is no way to live.

To close this chapter, I want to encourage you to do two exercises that will help you release yourself from the negative experiences in your past. You might be able to learn something from them and if you can, that's something to hold on to. On an emotional level, your past mistakes are not serving you. They will only make difficult situations in the present even harder to cope with. We have to be able to shift our focus away from the past and keep it rooted in the present. We have to think about the opportunities life will present us with rather than dwelling on the hardships we've had.

1 - Practice this 5-minute meditation

Close your eyes and take ten long, slow breaths. Focus on filling every corner of your body with air during your inhalation, and emptying yourself of it completely on your exhalation. Try to be fully present in this moment. Rid your mind of any thoughts that might be swarming around in your mind. If a thought does come your way, recognize it and let it pass. Then bring your focus back to your breathing. Keeping your mind from wandering takes practice but try to remember that your thoughts and feelings just want to be heard. You don't have to fight them, you just need to hear them and let them pass. Each time you feel distracted, bring your thoughts to a simpler place here in the present. Feel the air touching your upper lip as you exhale and focus on that physical sensation to bring you back to your meditative state in the here and now. The more often you do this, the easier it will become.

While you breathe, visualize the events from your past that are still haunting you. See your failures, your mistakes, and your embarrassing moments. Visualize yourself wrapping them up in a parcel. Imagine tying them to your back. Feel the weight of them dragging your shoulders into a slump. Feel the pressure on your spine. Imagine trying to walk forward with all that weight keeping you anchored to the spot. It feels like dragging a boulder. It feels like being pinned to the ground. Just breathe and visualize this. With this weight attached you to, imagine trying to run. Imagine trying to dance. Imagine trying to smile. Now picture yourself cutting those ties.

Imagine them snapping back, away from you. Feel how much lighter you become as you cut each tie. Feel how much movement you regain as your parcel becomes lighter and lighter. Feel your spine straighten and your chin lift. Feel the tension fall away from your muscles. Now leave the parcel behind you. Leave it right where it is and let yourself walk away from it. Let yourself be free of it and everything it contains. It isn't allowed to be with you anymore. You can move freely now knowing that the past is gone. It does not define you in the present. It cannot dictate how you feel. Breathe deeply for five or ten more breaths. Then open your eyes and smile.

2 - Make a list

If you were feeling low and someone offered you a five minute fix to lift your spirits, would you take it? This exercise can seem a bit silly but it can do just that. It's oddly effective when it comes to lifting your mood and keeping your mind from being overrun with negativity. This is a fantastic practice to adopt if your social anxiety is rooted in low self-esteem or poor self-image. It is also helpful when you hit a slump in your day or week.

Get a pen and a piece of paper. Write down 5 things you like about yourself. Don't let yourself get away with writing down any less than 5! Remember that being able to approve of yourself is a very important part of self-growth. Learning to accept ourselves, approve of ourselves, and love ourselves is a nonnegotiable part of getting over social anxiety. Remember that if you want to get over your anxiety completely, you've got to get to the root of the problem, not just mask it. You have to make a commitment to yourself if you want to achieve greater happiness and better self esteem. If you want to be able to walk into social situations with your head held high, you need to be able to withstand criticism and say goodbye to your insecurities. Writing lists like this one is like drinking a protein shake for your self-esteem. It can help you feel better immediately and the more you do it, the more easy you will find it to give yourself praise when it's due, and the better you will feel about yourself overall.

When you have finished writing your list, start a second one. This time write down 5 things you like about your life right now. Again, don't let yourself get away with any less than 5! You can write anything here, no matter how small, so don't worry if you don't have 5 things that are absolutely incredible. You might just love your dog or a piece of furniture in your house. You might like your job or your hobby. You might've just had a pretty decent day. Maybe you weren't stuck in traffic on the way home from work. Whatever it is, it will help you shift your focus onto positive things.

These exercises are great to do when you're feeling particularly low. They can really help turn your mood around and they're a lot more productive than reaching for a drink or scanning through your social media feeds. They will of course, get a lot easier the more you do them, but they never stop being effective.

Dealing With Unavoidable Social Situations

There are certain events in life that we just won't be able to escape.
So even if you're the King or Queen of Avoidance, you're going to
have to face the world at one time or another! Up to now, you have
learned a lot about navigating social situations and getting to the root
of your struggles with anxiety. But as these things will take time and
practice to fully sink in, this last section will offer you some advice
on coping with specific social situations that most of us will have to
face at some point in our lives.

1 - Weddings And Other Celebrations

Going to weddings is like entering Small Talk Central. If you hate
the idea of a stop and chat with one person, the idea of having
multiple stop and chats in rapid succession over the course of many
hours may seem like torture. Not only are you likely to see a bunch
of people you know and like, you're also likely to run into people
you'd rather not see. And on top of that, there are all those people
whose names you've forgotten and whose faces you can't place. Is
there anyone who doesn't find situations like these at least a little bit
daunting?

Start preparing for large social gatherings by putting them in
perspective. The thing about small talk is that it's unpredictable and
therefore, by nature, it's out of your control. Small talk isn't
something you can really prepare for. You won't know in advance
who you're going to end up chatting to or what they're going to want
to talk about. And as you know, the things that we can't predict or
control, are always going to ramp up our anxiety. The good news is
that, unless it's your wedding, the focus probably won't be on you!

Remember that people are rarely going to scrutinize the way you
look or what you say in conversations. The only person who's likely
to do that to you, is *you*. Everyone else is going to be too busy
thinking about themselves! So try not to be your worst enemy. Don't
be overly critical of yourself or get embarrassed by every tiny

conversational detail. Don't feel like you have to apologize for being alive! Conversations are fleeting and the majority of them are harmless. Do your best to just engage in the conversation rather than wondering when it's going to end. Remind yourself that you are not trapped. You can leave any time you want to. But also keep in mind that these brief conversations don't have to be taken so seriously. Most of them will be pretty insignificant. If you feel your anxiety building while you're talking to someone, try to slow down your thinking and focus on listening.

Remember that celebrations are supposed to be joyous occasions! Try to get something positive from the conversation by focusing on your enjoyment and intrigue, rather than on your anxiety. Let yourself lighten up.

If you're getting overly worked up about attending an event like this, look at yourself in the mirror and tell yourself that you're taking things a little too seriously. Life doesn't have to be such a drag. Tell your anxiety to take a hike for the night and try to loosen up. When we approach social situations in this light, it's astonishing how quickly we can actually get rid of our anxiety in the moment. Yes, you may still get a little bit jittery before you get there but eventually, there will come a time when you'll actually *enjoy* socializing. Practice makes perfect!

2 - Public Speaking

Whether you've been chosen to give a toast at a wedding or speak to a room full of colleagues at work, the rules are simple: Plan. Write. Rehearse. During the planning stage, try to keep your speech succinct. Start by writing down some bullet points about what you'd like to talk about. Then build around those. You want to get your message across in a genuine and professional way but that doesn't mean it has to be long or drawn out. A big part of public speaking is being engaging and it's easy to lose an audience by talking on and on without purpose. Say what you want to say and try to keep it brief. If you want to make a joke, keep it clean. If you don't want to joke around, don't! One of the most important elements of public speaking is sincerity, so try to relax and just be yourself. It's easier and more believable to be you than it is to try to be someone else!

Once you've written your speech, it's time to start rehearsing. Practicing a speech out loud (rather than just practicing in your head) is extremely important. You have to get used to how it feels in your mouth. Practicing will also help you to identify where your nerves are most likely to disturb you and how they will affect you. For instance, when you're nervous, do your hands shake? Does your voice quiver? Do you start to sweat? Whatever it is, you're better off rehearsing how to work around your nerves than you would be by going in cold turkey. You'll want to rehearse in front of a mirror and in front of a friend if possible. They you'll want to rehearse again! The more you practice your speech, the more comfortable you'll feel when the time comes.

Remember that it's okay to be nervous and it's okay to make mistakes. Just pick yourself back up, shake it off and start again. You are human and that is all people expect you to be. Most people get nervous when speaking in public so your audience is far more likely to be empathetic than judgmental. Try to keep that in mind to help you maintain perspective and keep your nerves at bay.

3 - Conflict And Confrontation

In our lives, we will all have experiences with other people that are going to be difficult. There are very few people in the world who enjoy conflict and confrontation, but we can't avoid these things all the time. Your conflict might be receiving disciplinary action at work or going through a break up at home. There may be times when you need to talk to your friends or family members about something they've done to upset you or vice versa. You might need to apologize for something you've said or done, or you might want someone to apologize to you.

Things like this can be extremely difficult because we can't hear what other people are thinking. We do our best to accurately gauge how others are feeling and we take certain cues from their behavior, but these things are not fool proof. Disagreements will happen, arguments will spin out of control. Human beings are passionate about how they think and feel, and not everyone will be open to other people's experiences.

In times of conflict, it's especially important to treat yourself kindly. Whether it's you who is at fault or not, you've still got to take care of number one. Often in difficult times we can focus on the wrong things. For instance we might try to *win* a fight rather than *end* it. We might decide that the person we're arguing with is being unreasonable or rude. We might blame everything on them. Or, you might be the type of person who is prone to taking all of the blame when in fact, the blame belongs to both of you. When our relationships are strained it is common for our view to get a bit skewed. If you are the type of person who tends to beat yourself up during times like these, it's extremely important to know when you're not at fault. Of course, it is equally important to know when you are. Being able to think clearly, rather than allowing your emotions to consume you, is vital.

Being in a conflict with someone does not have to be a catalyst for self-destruction. It does not always mean that everything has to change. Every conflict is not necessarily going to be catastrophic. Making mistakes does not mean that you are a terrible person; it just means you are a person. Doing something wrong does not mean that you are inherently bad. It doesn't feel good to know when we have caused someone else pain. But we can't let these moments shape how we feel about ourselves, nor can we allow our narcissistic defense come up swinging. In addition, when other people treat you wrongly, it might be worth taking some time to be curious about what's going on for them. Remember, it takes a strong person to be able to rise above conflict and view situations clearly. Relationships will inevitably go through ups and downs, but conflict doesn't have to mean the end of a relationship.

So how can you keep conflicts from spinning out of control? Start by taking some time to cool off. Positive resolutions are pretty hard to come by when everyone is still in the heat of the moment. If it's at all possible, tell the other person that you think it'd be best to take a little break and revisit this issue when you've both had some time to calm down. Explain that you do not mean to cause any added difficulty but that you feel like you need time to think. Then go away and try to make sense of things. Try to identify where things went wrong. Did you say things that you shouldn't have? Were there things the other person said that hurt your feelings? Was there something one of you took the wrong way; did your wires get crossed at some point? Is it possible that the whole thing is a misunderstanding? Most importantly, is it possible to reach a solution by compromising?

Once you've thought about it long enough, take some time to think about how you would like to proceed. Think about what you would like to get out of this. Do you want to resolve the conflict and repair the relationship? Do you want to end the relationship? Are you being reasonable or have you been swept up in the heat of the moment? If you want to resolve things, try not to go back to that person with guns blazing. Be reasonable. One thing that human beings tend to do is mirror one another. So, if you go in kicking and screaming, the other person is likely to do the same. If you go into the situation with a calm and empathic frame of mind, the other person is likely to match you. In that way, you can control the situation to some extent.

No matter what happens, try to maintain perspective. This moment will pass. Even if you've made a terrible mistake or you can't find a resolution to your problem, there will come a time when you will no longer hurt about it. Just remember not to use negative experiences as a weapon to beat yourself up with. Don't let moments of conflict dictate how you feel about socializing in general.

Getting The Most Out Of Life

As you approach the end of this book, take some time to reflect on your progress so far. Think about how you felt at the beginning of this book and make note of any changes you can identify in your thoughts and feelings. You might feel like you've really got a hold of your anxiety now, or you might feel like you're ready to take some small steps toward freeing yourself from it. We know that everyone is unique. Some of us find change exciting and easy, while others will have to put a little more time and energy into it. But regardless of who you are and what struggles you may possess, I hope that you are feeling more positive about what the future holds for you. I hope that you can see now that you do not have to live with social anxiety forever. You are strong enough break out of it. In the guided meditation I offered you not long ago, you were encouraged to break free from the negative experiences in your past. Now, you can also break the ties between you and anxiety. You don't have to carry it around with you forever. It doesn't have to be a dark cloud in your life anymore.

I hope that at this point, you are starting to get used to maintaining perspective as well as being patient with yourself. I hope that you are focusing on lifting yourself up rather than putting yourself down. Most of all, I hope that you will allow yourself to enjoy life a little bit more each day. I hope that you will soon feel solid enough in yourself to be able to find joy in social situations and in other people in general. I hope that you have learned to be kind to yourself, to give yourself credit for your triumphs, and to do your best to be light. I hope that you are taking plenty of time to reflect on your experiences so as to continue gaining a deeper understanding of your thoughts and feelings.

As one final exercise, I'd like to invite you to take the **Just Say Yes** challenge. Challenge yourself to accept every invitation you receive from other people. If you're used to saying no when your friends want you to go out for the night or you're a chronic no-show, taking this challenge means saying **YES** and meaning **YES** every time someone invites you out. It is too easy to become reclusive in these times dominated by screen-based communication. It is too easy to cancel. If you really want to break free of your anxiety and actually enjoy being around other people, I promise you that taking this final challenge, when you're ready to, will get you there.

As you move onto the next part of your journey, whatever that may be, remember to hold onto everything you've learned about yourself and your anxiety. As you progress through life, remember that you have the capacity to continue growing and changing for as long as you live. Life will present you with challenges and difficulties no matter who you are.

We will all go through ups and downs. But when it comes to anxiety, you are in control now. This is your life. Your time on earth is fleeting! Don't let your anxiety steal it from you.

Most of all, remember that life is for living. There's no time to waste!

46778575R00066

Made in the USA
San Bernardino, CA
16 March 2017